America Speaks
THE BIRTH OF THE NATION

VOLUME

7

UNDERPRIVILEGED

Duncan Clarke

GROLIER

For Compendium Publishing
Series editor: Don Gulbrandsen
Picture research: Sandra Forty
Design: Tony Stocks/Compendium Design
Artwork: Mark Franklin

Printed in China through Printworks Int. Ltd.

Library of Congress Cataloging-in-Publication Data
p. cm.
Summary: "Recounts the making of America until 1815 through
the eyes and voices of ordinary people"—Provided by publisher.
Includes indexes.

Contents: v. 1. Merchants / Angus Konstam—v. 2.
Manufacturers / Wayne Youngblood—v. 3. Armed Forces / Ian
Westwell—v. 4. Transporters / John Westwood—v. 5.
Professionals / Marcus Cowper—v. 6. Workers / Marcus Cowper
—v. 7. Underprivileged / Duncan Clarke—v. 8. Lawmen and
Lawbreakers / Philip Wilkinson—v. 9. Women / Jane Penrose—
v. 10. Children / Jane Penrose.

ISBN 0-7172-6030-5 (set : alk. paper)—ISBN 0-7172-6020-8 (v. 1
: alk. paper)—ISBN 0-7172-6021-6 (v. 2 : alk. paper)—ISBN 0-
7172-6022-4 (v. 3 : alk. paper)—ISBN 0-7172-6023-2 (v. 4 : alk.
paper)—ISBN 0-7172-6024-0 (v. 5 : alk. paper)—ISBN 0-7172-
6025-9 (v. 6 : alk. paper)—ISBN 0-7172-6026-7 (v. 7 : alk. paper)
—ISBN 0-7172-6027-5 (v. 8 : alk. paper)—ISBN 0-7172-6028-3
(v. 9 : alk. paper)—ISBN 0-7172-6029-1 (v. 10 : alk. paper)

1. United States—History—Colonial period, ca. 1600-1775—
Sources--Juvenile literature. 2. United States—History—
Revolution, 1775-1783—Sources—Juvenile literature. 3. United
States—History—1783-1815—Sources—Juvenile literature. 4.
United States—Social conditions—To 1865—Sources—
Juvenile literature. I. Konstam, Angus.

E188.A495 2005
973.2'5—dc22

2005040309

ACKNOWLEDGMENTS

The photographs in this book came
from the following sources. Numbers
refer to pages

Corbis: 3 (Historical Picture
Archive/Corbis, Corbis, & Bettmann/
Corbis), 4 (both Bettmann/Corbis), 9B
(Bettmann/Corbis), 17 (Bettmann/
Corbis), 25 (Historical Picture
Archive/Corbis), 26 (Christie's
Images/Corbis), 27 (Gianni Dagli
Orti/Corbis), 29 (Seattle Art
Museum/Corbis and Historical Picture
Archive/Corbis), 33, 36, 42, 43, 44
(Christel Gerstenberg/Corbis), 50B
(Austrian Archives/Corbis), 57, 58 (both
Bettmann/Corbis), 59 (Bettmann/
Corbis), 60, 61 (Bettmann/Corbis and
Lee Snider/Photo Images/Corbis), 62B
(below), 63 (Bettmann/Corbis), 64
(Corbis & Bettmann/Corbis), 65
(Bettmann/Corbis), 66
(Bettmann/Corbis).
Getty Images: 1, 5, 6 (Time Life
Pictures/Getty Images), 8 (National
Geographic/Getty Images), 9A, 10, 12
(both), 14 (both), 15 (Time Life
Pictures/Getty Images), 16 (both), 18,
19 (both), 20, 21, 22 (both), 23, 24, 28,
30 (both), 31, 32 (both), 34 (Time Life
Pictures/Getty Images), 35, 37, 38,
39,40, 41 (both), 45 (both), 46, 47 (Time
Life Pictures/Getty Images), 48 (both),
49, 50A, 51 (both), 52 (Time Life
Pictures/Getty Images), 53, 54, 55
(both), 56, 62A, 67, 68, 69 (Time Life
Pictures/Getty Images), 70, 71.

CONTENTS

For a long time it was believed that there were few poor and underprivileged people in early America. America was the land of opportunity. In the words of one English indentured servant it was "the best poor man's country." New immigrants might have found some hardships, but nothing that could not be overcome by hard work. Labor shortages and cheap land offered opportunities that meant everyone was well provided for—or were they? Work done by historians since the 1950s suggests that this rosy picture was a false one. Early America provided great prospects for thousands of people, but many immigrants struggled to survive in the New World. Add to that the plight of Native Americans and African slaves, and you realize that there was poverty and hardship for much of the population.

This volume will explore the lives of these disadvantaged

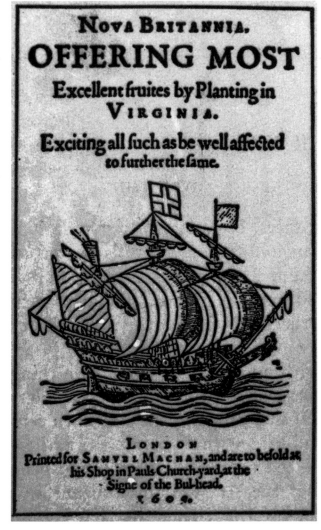

groups. It will look at topics such as how poor people reached America and their place in early American society. It will also consider how that society tried to both help them and control them. Many Native Americans, Africans, and European immigrants lived lives shaped by uncertainty, food shortages, charitable relief, and destitution. Their stories—and, wherever possible, their voices—are an important chapter in the history of early America. And these stories help us understand continuing social problems in America today.

Voices from the past

How can we know about poor people so far in the past? Historians study the traces of their lives left in documents written at the time or soon afterward such as books, letters, newspapers, court records, church and parish registers, and the notes of poor-relief officials. As far as possible in

LEFT: **A view of Jamestown, Virginia, in 1622. The first colonists experienced initial periods of great hardship and were constantly on guard against attack.**

BELOW LEFT: **A 1609 advertisement seeking colonists for Virginia. Promoters of the colonies boasted of fertile land and many opportunities, but their attempts to attract settlers were largely unsuccessful.**

BELOW: **Philadelphia, at the corner of Third and Market streets in 1799. American cities grew quickly and soon attracted the poor from the countryside.**

this book we have tried to feature "voices" from these old documents commenting on what they saw or thought or experienced. However, there are notable gaps in the historical record, and these gaps themselves can tell us something about the past. As is often the case, we know a lot about the thoughts and opinions of the wealthy and successful but very little of the direct voices of the poor and under-privileged. The documents available may be about the poor and even record some of the names and glimpses of their lives, but with a few rare exceptions they were not written by poor people.

Recipients of poor relief and charity were not often consulted about their opinions and experiences; and even if they were, their answers were not usually written down. Poor workers were too busy struggling to survive to have time to write an autobiography, even if they had the resources or ability to do so. The few letters they may have written survive only in exceptional cases. It is interesting to compare these gaps in the historical record with the comparatively large number of testimonies left by ex-slaves. In their case the growing abolitionist movement provided both the means for publication and the audience for the works. Extraordinary events such as the Revolutionary War also attracted attention and interest in the "voices" and experiences of participants. Sadly poverty, poor relief, and the daily struggles of unskilled workers to feed their families were simply too much a part of everyday life to attract much attention.

Land of opportunity

Colonial and postrevolutionary America pictured itself as the land of opportunity. It was a place where the old inequalities, religious bigotry, and class boundaries that held back progress in England were thrown aside. It was a place where honest hard work was rewarded by comfort and material security. Humble people, whether farmers or tradesmen, could succeed beyond anything they could hope for in Europe. The best-known promoter of this view was Benjamin Franklin. In 1772 he wrote a pamphlet promoting the benefits of America to would-be migrants.

"Land being cheap in that country…hearty young laboring men, who understand the husbandry of corn and cattle…may easily establish themselves there. A little money saved of the good wages they receive there, while they work for others, enables them to buy the land and begin their plantation, in which they are assisted by the goodwill of their neighbors, and some credit. Multitudes of poor people from England, Ireland, Scotland, and Germany, have by this means in a few years become wealthy farmers, who, in their own countries, where all the lands are fully occupied, and the wages of labor low, could never have emerged from the poor condition wherein they were born.

"…From the salubrity [healthiness] of the air, the healthiness of the climate, the plenty of good provisions, and the encouragement to early marriages by the certainty of subsistence in cultivating the earth, the increase of inhabitants by natural generation is very rapid in America…hence there is a continual demand for more artisans of all the necessary and useful kinds, to supply those cultivators of the earth with houses, and with furniture and utensils… Tolerably good workmen in any of those mechanic arts are sure to find employ, and to be well paid for their work….If they are poor, they begin first as servants or journeymen; and if they are sober, industrious, and frugal, they soon become masters, establish themselves in business, marry, raise families, and become respectable citizens."

Franklin was, of course, writing propaganda and trying to persuade hard-working people to better themselves in the new United States. At the same time, he sincerely believed that opportunity and good fortune were there for the taking—provided that immigrants worked hard and lived wisely. Before the Revolution he published a popular series of almanacs—small collections of information and wisdom—called *Poor Richard* and *Poor Richard Improved*. Throughout them a frequent refrain was that of self-improvement and discipline:

"If we are industrious we shall never starve; for, as Poor Richard says, At the working Man's House Hunger looks in, but dares not enter. Nor will the Bailiff or the Constable enter, for Industry pays Debts, while Despair encreaseth them, says Poor Richard….What though you have found no Treasure, nor has any rich Relation left you a Legacy, Diligence is the Mother of Good-luck, as Poor Richard says, and God gives all Things to Industry."

However, the repetition of these themes in Franklin's writing reveals something important: Too many of his fellow citizens were failing to achieve the prosperity he expected of them. Franklin was writing about how things could be and should be rather than how they really turned out. Unlike many later commentators who took his words at face value, Franklin was aware that many Americans lived in poverty. As we will see later, he had firm views about why this was and about what should be done. He was a key figure in changing attitudes toward poor relief in the eighteenth century.

Who were the poor?

Who were the poor and underprivileged groups in early America, and where did they come from? The first colonists and others who established tiny footholds on the new continent experienced periods of great hardship. Some colonies failed altogether, while many of the earliest arrivals in others quickly died from disease and hunger. Once crops could be harvested and the harsh winter passed, conditions for most improved. As all students know, Thanksgiving still commemorates the Pilgrims' survival of their first year of challenges in the new colony.

For the Native Americans the first settlers encountered, the situation is more complex. Scholars debate whether or not it is right to consider them poor.

BELOW: **William Penn (1644-1718), the English Quaker founder of Philadelphia, is shown meeting with Dutch colonists on his first visit to America.**

LEFT: **Archaeologists have been able to uncover many details about daily life in the early colonies. Here excavations take place at Jamestown, Virginia.**

RIGHT: **In the 1700s New York was still a small town with settlers dependent on farming for survival. Here, in a romantic view of what was in fact a very hard way of life, two women use a balance-pole well to raise water for their livestock.**

BELOW RIGHT: **A view of Brooklyn, New York, in 1816. Farm animals competed for space in the unpaved streets with pedestrians and horse-drawn carriages.**

They recognize that Native Americans had very different ideas about material objects and relationships between people and land than the settlers. Native groups moved around freely within a range of habitats. By custom they used certain products of the land, and they established trade patterns with neighboring tribes. In some cases they gained prestige by giving away material goods rather than keeping them as wealth. A famous example is the potlatch of the Pacific Northwest tribes, a feast in which chiefs generously gave away their wealth as gifts to show their power.

But as European influence spread, Native American life patterns quickly collapsed. War, new material goods, disease, and lost access to traditional lands all brought change. Soon, food shortages, poor health, short life spans, and other signs of poverty became the norm for surviving Native Americans. Most tribes struggled to adapt to, and survive, their changing circumstances.

In colonial and postrevolutionary America the vast majority of African Americans were slaves. As slaves they were considered property. According to the standards of that time it made no sense to describe them as poor. Slaves were usually forbidden from owning any property, and any small items they

accumulated were subject to the wishes and whims of their masters. Their goods and even their family members could be seized and disposed of at any time.

In later decades, as the abolitionist movement gained strength, there was great debate over the slaves' living conditions. A key claim of proslavery forces in the South was that life, work, and living conditions were much better for slaves than they were for factory workers in the crowded slum cities in Europe. George Fitzhugh, one of the most widely published Southern supporters of slavery, claimed in the 1850s that:

> "Slavery here relieves him from a far more cruel slavery in Africa, or from idolatry and cannibalism, and every brutal vice and crime that can disgrace humanity; and that it christianizes, protects, supports and civilizes him; that it governs him far better than free laborers at the North are governed."

Today we can recognize (as did forward-thinking people in the eighteenth century) that much of the wealth of the American colonies came from maintaining a large slave population. For the few Africans and African Americans

who managed to gain their freedom, life was uncertain and difficult, and they were often among the poorest and most underprivileged people. As the prominent African American abolitionist Frederick Douglass argued:

> "Though no longer a slave, he is in a thralldom grievous and intolerable, compelled to work for whatever his employer is pleased to pay him, swindled out of his hard earnings by money orders redeemed in stores, compelled to pay the prince of an acre of ground for its use during a single year, to pay four times more than a fair price for a pound of bacon and to be kept upon the narrowest margin between life and starvation."

Indentured servants

Slaves were not the only "unfree" and underprivileged workers in early America. Early in the colonial era white people brought from Britain, Ireland, and other European countries as indentured servants outnumbered African slaves. An indenture was a contract under which the signer agreed to work as a servant for the other party for a given number of years. In return the contract spelled out the benefits the

servant would receive. Wage labor was not common at this time. Purchasing indentured servants was the main way for colonists to get the workers they needed.

For the servants conditions were often harsh, and complaints were frequent. Elizabeth Sprigs's 1756 letter to her father is typical of surviving documents from the period.

"What we unfortunate English People suffer here is beyond the probability of you in England to Conceive, let it suffice that I one of the unhappy Number, am toiling almost Day and Night, and very often in the Horses drudgery, with only this comfort that you Bitch you do not halfe enough, and then tied up and whipp'd to that Degree that you'd not serve an Animal, scarce any thing but Indian Corn and Salt to eat and that even begrudged nay many Negroes are better used, almost naked no shoes nor stockings to wear, and the comfort after slaving during Masters pleasure, what rest we can get is to [w]rap ourselves up in a Blanket and lie upon the Ground, this is the deplorable Condition your poor Betty endures, and now I beg if you have any Bowels of Compassion left show it by sending me some Relief, Clothing is the principal thing wanting, which if you should condescend to, may easily send them to me by any of the ships bound to Baltimore."

Some in Britain saw the indenture system as a convenient and cheap way of ridding the country of poor people. These people, otherwise, would have been entitled to costly assistance. That the colonies were eager for workers was often a minor concern. This official view of the Americas as an easy dumping ground for the unwanted was even more

apparent in the sending of many convicts and war prisoners to America. Convicts were often bound as servants for periods of 18 years or more. They were subjected to particularly harsh treatment that many did not survive.

The final group of "unfree" laborers to arrive in America was known as "redemptioners." They traveled under a slightly different arrangement than

standard indentured servants. Redemptioners usually emigrated as family groups. The terms of their contracts with ship captains allowed them a short time (usually about 14 days) after arriving in America to pay off, or "redeem," their transport costs. Usually they had no money and no relatives or friends in the port who were willing or able to help them. Their only option was to bind some

or all of the family as indentured servants and have their new master pay the transportation costs. If arrangements were not made in the given time, the ship captain would usually indenture them to the highest bidders. The number of redemptioners, who were mostly from an area of Germany called the Palatine, increased sharply through the second half of the eighteenth century.

What became of these indentured servants once their period of service was complete? Did they, as Franklin and many other hoped, benefit from the discipline, local knowledge, and contacts gained during their years of service? Did they soon establish themselves in a life of hard work but relative prosperity? Some did, and there are a number of famous and often-cited examples of

BELOW: **Early settlers fortified their colonies for protection against rival European powers and pirates as well as hostile Native Americans. This 1673 engraving shows the settlement of Charles Town (now Charleston) in South Carolina, with impressive city walls.**

NEW YORK

By the close of the eighteenth century New York was already a large urban center with the associated problems of poverty and crime.

TOP: **Broad Street, Wall Street, and City Hall around 1797.**

ABOVE: **Parades, such as this event on July 26, 1788, marking the ratification of the Constitution, provided a welcome break from the struggles of daily life for the urban poor.**

former servants who rose to the highest ranks of colonial society. However, they were exceptions, and most historians believe that only about one in ten indentured servants found success in the New World. Of the rest many died before their service was completed, often during their first months in America. The Atlantic crossing weakened the poor travelers' malnourished bodies, and they often fell prey to new diseases. Eventually most of the survivors swelled the ever-growing ranks of the poor and needy in colonial towns and cities.

Poor relief

Today we tend to think of welfare, food stamps, and similar programs as measures that emerged in the twentieth century in response to the Great Depression. In reality some form of public assistance—also called relief—to the poor has been a feature of American life since the earliest colonial days. It was seen as a moral, civic, and religious duty for the community to assist those who were unable to take care of themselves. Local taxes were raised to support the poor, and such aid was seen as one of the key duties of civic leaders. As today, there were constant financial pressures that limited what the community would, and could, provide. As a result there were lively debates about exactly who was entitled to—or deserving of—assistance.

The foundation of poor relief in colonial America was a system that operated back in England. It was based on the Elizabethan Poor Law of 1601. At the system's heart was what was called "out relief" or "outdoor relief," under which the poor were assisted within the community by small payments or gifts of food or clothing to meet particular needs. Or arrangements were made for them to be housed and fed by a citizen for a specified, usually short, period of time. Children were usually bound out as servants to someone who housed and educated them. To qualify for this relief, the person in question had to be a legitimate inhabitant of the town. They qualified by being born there or by completing a period of service there. All other people—even if they had lived in the town for many years—were liable to be sent away or "warned out" to look for help elsewhere. Often people had to return to their place of birth or somewhere else where they could establish a better claim to aid. Because of this potential expense of providing public assistance, towns were very wary of admitting strangers who were unable to demonstrate that they had adequate means of support.

Urban poverty

By the middle of the eighteenth century the cost of caring for the growing number of poor people in the expanding cities of Boston, Newport, Philadelphia, New York, and Charles Town (Charleston) was rising rapidly. The desire to reduce these costs became tied in with a moral debate about the causes of and cures for poverty. In a society in which the successful believed that they had become so by their own—albeit God-given—talents and hard work, it was a short step to argue that the poor were mostly poor through their own faults. In some cases this was clearly not the case, but more people began to distinguish between the "deserving" and the "undeserving" poor. While the "deserving" were entitled to relief assistance, it was argued that the "undeserving" poor needed to be reformed. Relief would merely maintain them in their present state, which was the result of laziness, drunkenness, and so on. But a formal system of reform and discipline could change them into productive, hard-working citizens.

For both the deserving and the undeserving it was believed that strict supervision would not only aid their recovery but also reduce costs. Almshouses (for the "deserving" poor) and workhouses (for the "undeserving" poor, though in practice the differences were unclear) were built in response to this changed approach to poor relief. It is not surprising that scholars have documented ways in which the gender and race of applicants influenced decisions about who received relief and what type of relief was given. Free black men and women, for example, were far more likely to be warned out of a community than to be granted assistance in a time of need.

However, poor men and women were not simply passive and permanent aid recipients. Instead, they took action to protect their own interests. They took advantage of aid in the form of out relief or almshouses where they were available and necessary, though they usually avoided having their choices controlled by relief officials. For most people being so poor that relief was needed was a constant concern but not a constant state. Instead, they moved in and out of poverty. At some times they were better off, maybe because of work or marriage. But there always was the danger of falling back into poverty because of old age, illness, injury, harsh weather, and many of the other uncertainties of life. Like their better-off friends, they enjoyed taverns, attended churches, worked where they could, married, raised children, and had their joys and disasters. Underlying all this was a constant awareness of life's insecurity and their vulnerability to minor setbacks that could throw them back into the poor-relief system.

The first British attempts to colonize the American mainland began at the end of the sixteenth century following the grant of a patent (royal permission) to Sir Walter Raleigh by Queen Elizabeth in 1584.

Establishing a viable colony on the coast of North America required both careful planning and good fortune. The initial settlement and early years of any colony were periods of great danger and uncertainty. The settlers had yet to secure reliable food supplies, were exposed to a harsh climate and new diseases, and were vulnerable to attack by Native Americans. The earliest attempts, at Roanoke, ended in failure. The first years of the more successful colonies at Jamestown and Massachusetts Bay were marked by periods of severe food shortage and high death rates. Roanoke is now primarily remembered for the mysterious disappearance of the 90 men, 17 women, and 9 children established on the island in 1587. When John White's supply mission returned from England after a delay of three years, only the overgrown settlement remained—as described in the panel on the next page.

The Virginia colony established at Jamestown in 1607 almost suffered a similar fate in its first year, as John Smith's *Generall Historie of Virginia* (1624) recalls:

> "Being thus left to our fortunes, it fortuned that within ten days scarce ten among us could either go or well stand, such extreme weakness and sickness oppressed us….With this lodging and diet, our extreme toil in bearing and planting palisades so strained and bruised us, and our continual labor in the extremity of the heat had so weakened us, as were cause sufficient to have made us as miserable in our native country, or any other place in the world. From May to September, those that escaped lived upon sturgeon, and sea crabs. Fifty in this time we buried….But now was all our

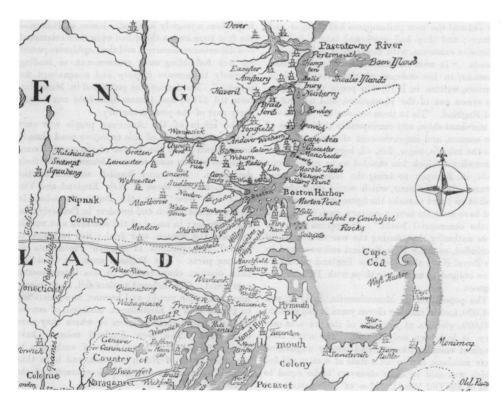

LEFT: **On December 21, 1620, the Pilgrims make camp at Plymouth Colony after their arrival in America. Their ship, the *Mayflower*, lies anchored in the bay behind them; a Native American watches secretly from the trees.**

BELOW LEFT: **Some years later the colonies were flourishing. This is a map of colonial New England from about 1700.**

provision spent, the sturgeon gone, all helps abandoned, each hour expecting the fury of the savages; when God, the Patron of all good endeavors in that desperate extremity so changed the hearts of the savages that they brought such plenty of their fruits and provision as no man wanted....We were at sea five months, where we both spent our victual and lost the opportunity of the time and season to plant, by the unskillful presumption of our ignorant transporters, that understood not at all what they undertook....And now, the winter approaching, the rivers became so covered with swans, geese, ducks, and cranes that we daily feasted with good bread, Virginia peas, pumpions [pumpkins], and putchamins [persimmons], fish, fowl, and diverse sorts of wild beasts as fat as we could eat them."

Starving time

However, their problems were not yet over. In the winter that became known as the "starving time" following Smith's departure in 1609, only 60 of the original 214 settlers survived. New arrivals sent over by the Virginia Company replenished the population, but in the early decades the inhabitants of Jamestown continued to be threatened by epidemics, poor farming techniques, conflicts with their Native American neighbors, and the inadequate policies of the Virginia Company. By the time King James revoked the company's charter and brought the colony under direct control in 1624, only about one thousand of the six to ten thousand settlers had survived.

ABOVE: **Drawing by John White of Native Americans observed during Sir Walter Raleigh's expedition to Virginia.**

DESERTED ROANOAKE

Writing in the English of the day, John White recorded that the Roanoake settlement was overgrown and in ruins, with abandoned objects scattered around and only a cryptic message left behind:

"We passed toward the place where they were left in sundry houses, but we found the houses taken downe, and the place very strongly enclosed with a high palisado [palisade, or fence] of great trees, with cortynes [cordon, or line of defense] and flankers very Fort-like, and one of the chief trees or posts at the right side of the entrance had the barke taken off, and 5 foote from the ground in fair Capital letters was grauen [engraved] CROATOAN without any crosse or signe of distress; this done, we entered into the palisado, where we found many bars of Iron, two pigges [pig, or crude metal casting] of Lead, four iron fowlers [guns], Iron sacker-shotte, and such like heavie things, thrown here and there, almost overgrown with grasse and weedes. From thence wee went along by the water side, towards the point of the Creek to see if we could find any of their boats or Pinnisse, but we could perceive no signe of them, nor any of the last Falkons [falchion, or sword] and small Ordinance [weapons] which were left with them, at my departure from them. At our returne from the Creek, some of our Sailors meeting us, tolde us that they had found where divers[e] chests had been hidden, and long since digged up againe and broken up, and much of the goods in them spoiled and scattered about, but nothing left, of such things as the Savages knew any use of, undefaced."

The *Mayflower* Pilgrims

Like their predecessors in Jamestown, the Pilgrims on the *Mayflower* went through a period of great hardship and insecurity that threatened the survival of the colony.

The first Thanksgiving marked only the end of the early phase of a three-year struggle to build a successful settlement.

The *Mayflower* Pilgrims, who were Puritan refugees from religious persecution in England, landed at Plymouth in December 1620. This was an unfavorable date because winter had already started. There was no hope of growing crops to supplement their limited food supplies. Up to 90 percent of the local Wampanoag

Indians had been killed by epidemic diseases between 1616 and 1618, and the Pilgrims were able to shelter in the abandoned native villages and raid their food caches. Nevertheless only half survived that first harsh winter. The spring bought plentiful fish and an alliance with the remaining Wampanoag, who taught the settlers how to harvest and cook local crops such as corn, squash, and pumpkin.

According to tradition the first Thanksgiving meal was celebrated together with the Pilgrims' Wampanoag allies in November 1621. Soon afterward rations had to be cut in half as winter set in once again. Thirty new settlers arrived on the ship *Fortune* without any further supplies, straining the scanty resources even more. The grim period of the "starvation time" was under way. Somehow the Pilgrim provisions had to

ABOVE: **Boatloads of people wave farewell to the *Mayflower* as the ship leaves Plymouth, England, for America on September 6, 1620.**

LEFT: **The signatures of Pilgrims who crossed the Atlantic on the *Mayflower* shown on the "Mayflower Compact," the first written framework of government in America. Included are William Brewster, William Bradford, Myles Standish, and Edward Winslow.**

last not only through the harsh winter but until the harvest was ripe the following August. By May 1622 their food stocks were nearly gone. Hunting and fishing provided some protein, but inexperience and lack of proper equipment limited the Pilgrims' success. Edward Winslow, one of the Pilgrim leaders and later a governor of the colony, was forced to travel 150 miles north to beg for aid from English ships on the Maine coast. By the time he returned, many settlers were weak from starvation, and the new rations were barely sufficient to maintain the colony. The failure of the long-awaited harvest in 1622 left the situation in crisis. Winslow stated:

"And indeed, had we not been in a place where divers[e] sorts of shell fish may be taken with the hand, we must have perished."

They also gathered wild berries, grapes, groundnuts, and strawberries, and with the help of their Wampanoag allies gradually became better at food gathering and hunting.

Some additional help came with the arrival of the ship *Discovery*, en route back to England from Virginia. Although it brought little food, the Pilgrims were able to stock up on trade goods such as beads and knives, which they exchanged for food with nearby Native Americans. In early 1623 they outfitted a small boat for fishing and caught enough cod to provide a vital boost to their diet. William Bradford, governor of the Pilgrim colony for more than 30 years, wrote of this time saying:

"By the time our corn is planted, our victuals [food supplies] are spent, not knowing at night where to have a bite in the morning, and have neither bread nor corn for 3 or 4 months together; yet bear our wants with cheerfulness, and rest on Providence."

For days at a time they survived on a rations of just a few grains of corn per person. All hopes were pinned on the fall harvest. Prospects looked bleak when a drought starting in mid-June began to dry up the corn. In mid-July, after a desperate assembly to pray for God's mercy, rain began to fall. A few days later the ships *Anne* and *Little James* bought both 65 new settlers and a plentiful stock of provisions. With the first successful harvest the following month the starving times were over and the future of the colony at last secured.

BELOW: **Public worship by the Pilgrims at Plymouth colony.**

The Native Americans first encountered by the English settlers were mostly Algonquin. Consisting of many different tribes, they were members of a language family that was scattered across a vast territory.

Shaped roughly like a triangle, the Algonquin tribal lands extended from what is now North Carolina to the St. Lawrence River in Canada and from the Atlantic Ocean to the Rocky Mountains. Most tribes grew corn and other crops using slash-and-burn agriculture, in which land is cleared by cutting down trees and brush and setting fire to the waste masterial. They supplemented their crops with hunting and food gathering.

Scholars have debated whether it is right to use European concepts such as poverty to describe these people. Native Americans had a very different understanding of their relationship with material objects and their environment.

A French missionary, Chrestien Le Clercq, quoted the arguments of a Micmac chief in 1676:

"I beg thee now to believe that, all miserable as we seem in thine eyes, we consider ourselves nevertheless much happier than thou in this, that we are very content with the little that we have; and believe also once for all, I pray, that thou deceivest thyself greatly if thou thinkest to persuade us that thy country is better than ours."

However, there is no doubt that the rapid changes in colonial America left Native Americans poor and one of the most oppressed groups in the new society. In just a few decades disease, war, and cultural breakdown changed Native American societies from independent, self-sustaining communities to small dependent groups, scattered bands, and isolated individuals. A rare indigenous perspective on the drastic changes comes from Miantonomo (died 1643), a Narragansett chief in a speech urging unity prior to an attack on the colonists:

"Brothers, we must be as one as the English are, or we shall all be destroyed. You know our fathers had plenty of deer and skins and our plains were full of game and turkeys, and our coves and rivers were full of fish. But, brothers, since these Englishmen have seized our country, they have cut down the grass with scythes, and the trees with axes. Their cows and horses eat up the grass, and their hogs spoil our bed of clams; and finally we shall all starve to death; therefore, stand not in your own light, I ask you, but resolve to act like men. All the sachems [chiefs] both to the east and the west have joined with us, and we are resolved to fall upon them at a day appointed, and therefore I come secretly to you, cause you can persuade your Indians to do what you will."

LEFT: Despite the collapse of Native American culture in the face of epidemics and other challenges, early Christian missionaries attracted only a few converts. John Eliot (1604–1690), one of the first missionaries to work among the native tribes, is shown around 1645.

BELOW: A Mohawk village in New York state, shown around 1780.

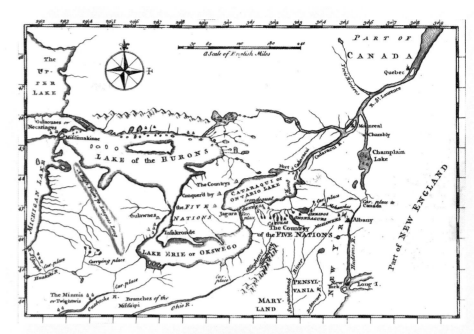

THE FIVE NATIONS

A map showing the country of the Five Nations, or Iroquois, from about 1650. This area now includes New York as well as part of Canada and lakes Huron, Michigan, Superior, Erie, and Ontario. The Five Nations was a league of tribes—the Mohawk, Oneida, Onondaga, Cayuga, and Seneca—that had formerly fought with each other. Tradition has it that the founders were Hiawatha and Dekanawida. Set up in the late sixteenth century, possibly in response to European conflict, they were allies of the British but were split by the Revolution, the Oneida siding with the Americans.

Virgin soil epidemics

Even as the first colonies were being established on the coast, diseases were wiping out Native American populations. This had also happened during the previous century in Central and South America. There were a series of what scientists call "virgin soil epidemics" in which previously unknown diseases spread rapidly through vulnerable populations with no natural immunity. Scholars suggest that there were two major epidemics that affected the Northeastern tribes during the

ABOVE: **Initial contacts between the Pilgrims and Native Americans were friendly, as this image of a shared meal in about 1625 illustrates—but the settlers brought disease and conflict that would kill many of the natives.**

ABOVE RIGHT: **Native Americans cure meat for the coming winter in about 1565. Shared Native American knowledge of hunting and agriculture was vital to the early settlers adapting to life in the New World.**

seventeenth century. The first, which may have been bubonic plague, yellow fever, or hepatitis, struck coastal peoples in 1616. This epidemic led to the empty Wampanoag villages discovered by the Pilgrims in 1620. In 1633 an outbreak of smallpox virtually wiped out

Algonquin and Iroquois tribes across a huge area. The combined effect of these diseases reduced the population of most Northeastern tribes by 80 to 95 percent. It is impossible for us to comprehend the epidemics' devastating impact on Native American life. The diseases were especially harmful because they arrived at the same time as the colonists—alien people with a very different way of life. John Josselyn describes the sad state of Native Americans encountered during his two visits to New England in the 1630s:

"Not long before the English came to this Countrey, happened a great mortality amongst them, especially where the English afterwards planted, the East and Northern parts were sore smitten with the Contagion; first the plague,

afterwards when the English came by the small pox, the three Kingdoms or Sagamoreships of the Massachusetts were very populous…but by the plague were brought from 30,000 to 300. There are not many now to the Eastward, the Pequots were destroyed by the English: the Mohacks are about five hundreds."

Conflict with settlers

Initial contacts between Native Americans and colonists were usually friendly, with the natives teaching the new arrivals how to survive in the New World. Unfortunately relations soon broke down. Europeans often demanded land and religious conversion from the native tribes. Men heavily outnumbered women in most of the early colonies and attempts to abduct native women were

frequent, as were robbery and slave raiding. Native Americans often retaliated, which prompted similar violence from colonists. Mutual distrust and fear led to regular small-scale conflict and occasional larger outbreaks such as the Pequot War and King Phillip's War. Hundreds of Native American women and children were massacred in numerous incidents. Different tribes were caught up in the rivalry between France and England that was stimulated by growing European demand for American furs. Firearms sold by settlers to native allies were often used in attempts to wipe out rival tribes. Population numbers already drastically reduced by disease declined further.

Throughout the seventeenth century Native American culture broke down or changed. Settler demand for furs was met by a growing focus on trapping—at the expense of farming, hunting, and food gathering. As a result some tribes starved. In exchange for furs Native Americans received cloth, beads, iron nails, knives, brass kettles, and firearms, all of which helped change lifestyles. Traders also supplied huge quantities of alcohol, with far-reaching social and health consequences. Intertribe co-operation broke down in the face of the new emphasis on trading. In some areas individual rights to land or food resources were asserted and enforced. Religious traditions were abandoned, and some conversions to Christianity took place along with the emergence of new, hybrid religious practices.

As the English colonies expanded, isolated groups of Native Americans remained behind the frontier. They adapted as best they could, either in separate communities on small reser-

vations or as individuals on the margins of colonial life. In the following centuries most were displaced and moved several times. Others, however, were able to remain and rebuild some part of their tribal identity thanks to a new lifestyle based on fur trading. Within this general overview there were many local stories of resistance and tragedy as tribes dwindled from thousands to a handful of individuals. Some tribes survived into the modern era, but many others live on only in history books.

Through most of the seventeenth and eighteenth centuries around two thirds of all white immigrants to the American colonies were indentured servants. In this section we will consider what it meant to be an indentured servant, what kinds of people came to America this way, and what their experiences were.

An indenture was a legal document under which one person agreed to be a servant to another person for some period. The period was usually four or five years, but sometimes was as long as seven years. In return the servant received specified benefits. These benefits usually included the cost of his or her passage to America, food and lodging during the service, and sometimes a small sum of money or

piece of land once the service was completed. The earliest of this type of indenture dates from around 1620. A second important type, which we will look at in more detail later, was applied to poor children already in America. The colonial indenture system developed from the practice of hiring servants in England but was more formal and more standardized. The system was changed to fit the needs of the expanding colonies

and took into account the expense of reaching America. It provided planters and other settlers with a vital source of labor they needed to develop their land.

The indenture system was essential to the prosperity of Virginia and the other southern colonies, but it was less crucial in New England. An anonymous English commentator in the middle of the seventeenth captured this difference noting:

> "Virginia thrives by keeping many servants and these in strict obedience. New England conceit [believe] they and their children can do enough and so rarely have above one servant."

Without the use of indentures there was no practical way for the poor of Britain to reach the Americas and the opportunities that supposedly waited there for them. Leading colonists also saw the indentured servants as a future white population to balance the ever-growing numbers of black slaves. However, indentures reduced men and women to goods that could be shipped at

LEFT: **A modern painting depicting life on a Virginia plantation in the early years of the seventeenth century. Farm workers harvest tobacco, while a ship lies anchored on the river behind them. In the early colonial period many indentured servants ended up laboring on plantations. Later slaves would take over.**

BELOW LEFT: **This indenture document is dated 1771 and agrees an apprenticeship of 11 years five months.**

BELOW: **"High Life below Stairs" shows a party being held in the servant's quarters in about 1820.**

a profit. Indentures were usually signed with ship's captain or their agents. Once the ship arrived in an American port, indentures were transferred through an auction or other sale to planters requiring labor. Like slaves the "surplus" poor became a commodity bought and sold for profit. In the process many suffered considerable hardship, and few lived to enjoy the prospects that Ben Franklin and others promised to hard-working migrants.

Trading in poverty

There were many poor people struggling to survive in the growing cities of seventeenth- and eighteenth-century Britain. But it is doubtful that many considered the drastic step of emigrating to unknown prospects in the colonies as a better alternative. Ship captains employed professional recruiting agents, known as "spirits," to sign people to indentures. The spirits hung around taverns and markets looking for people down on their luck or desperate to escape some problem. Then the spirits convinced the people to sign with tall tales and false promises of riches in the colonies.

Inevitably many of those who signed later tried to go back on their agreement. There were regular complaints that children, runaway wives and servants, and drunk or dim-witted people were being exploited and even kidnapped. Authorities in London and other major ports set up registers of indenture agreements in an attempt to curb these abuses. Taking children raised special concern. In 1645 the British Parliament required London port authorities to search all vessels in the Thames River that were about to leave for the colonies. It ordered all officers:

"To be very diligent in apprehending all such persons as are faulty in this kind, either in stealing, selling, buying, inveigling, purloining, conveying, or receiving Children so stolne [stolen]."

RUN away, the 23d of this Inftant *January*, from *Silas Crifpin* of *Burlington*, Taylor, a Servant Man named *Jofeph Morris*, by Trade a Taylor, aged about 22 Years, of a middle Stature, fwarthy Complexion, light gray Eyes, his Hair clipp'd off, mark'd with a large pit of the Small Pox on one Cheek near his Eye, had on when he went away a good Felt Hat, a yelowifh Drugget Coat with Pleits behind, an old Ozenbrigs Veft, two Ozenbrigs Shirts, a pair of Leather Breeches handfomely worm'd and flower'd up the Knees, yarn Stockings and good round toe'd Shoes Took with him a large pair of Sheers crack'd in one of the Bows, & mark'd with the Word [*Savoy*]. Whoever takes up the faid Servant, and fecures him fo that his Mafter may have him again, fhall have *Three Pounds* Reward befides reafonable Charges, paid by me *Silas Crifpin.*

RUNAWAYS

As with missing slaves eighteenth-century newspapers often carried advertisements noting details of runaway servants and offering a reward for their return. The following ad ran in the *Pennsylvania Gazette* in 1760:

"Run away last Night from William Scott, of this City, an Apprentice Boy, named Job Goodman, by Trade a Taylor, about 16 or 17 years old, a well looking Boy, tall and slim, has a very innocent Look and Speech, wears brown Hair, tied behind with a black Ribbon (but it is likely he will cut it off, for he has got a blue and white Cotton Cap). Had on when he went away, a light coloured Cloth Coat and Breeches, with yellow carved Metal Buttons, black Jacket, check Shirt, and a pair of Silver Buckles on his Shoes. Whoever takes up the said Apprentice, and brings him home to his said Master shall be rewarded with Forty Shillings, and all reasonable Charges, paid by William Scott."

Once on board a ship, the would-be migrants were provided with new clothing and basic rations. A close watch was kept to see that none ran away before the ship was ready to sail. The voyage, like all Atlantic crossings of this time, took a harsh toll. Conditions on board ship were terrible. Many of the migrants were already malnourished and in poor health. Food was low quality and insufficient, and disease was a constant threat. The death of 10 to 20 percent of the indentured passengers was typical. More would die if there were an outbreak of smallpox or dysentery during the eight- to ten-week voyage. Nonetheless it is estimated that somewhere between 200,000 and 300,000 indentured servants survived to reach the American colonies before the end of the colonial era.

Indentured servants in the colonies had lower status and were underprivileged relative to their masters and other free citizens. But they differed from slaves in that they had a legal status and a carefully defined set of rights and duties. Both the law and the customs of the day set boundaries on how they could be treated. Masters who exceeded these through excessive beatings or sexual misconduct with female servants faced both public condemnation and, in some cases, legal action. Under criminal law servants were entitled to the same protection and subjected to the same penalties as free men and women. Their situation differed because of their contractual obligations to their master and in the behavior that was seen as a breach of these duties. They—or rather their contracts—could be sold without their consent, transferring them to a new place and a new master. Offenses such as attempting to run away were punished by extending the length of their service. Permission from the master was required before a servant could marry, and a servant having a baby was usually made to serve a longer period to compensate the master for the time lost during the pregnancy.

Servants or slaves?

At first demand for indentured servants was strongest in the plantation colonies of the South. There they were worked as field hands growing staple crops such as tobacco and sugar. As more African slaves were imported in the late seventeenth century, planters found that it was more profitable to use slaves as field hands. Usually they kept a smaller number of indentured servants employed as craftsmen, supervisors, and housekeepers. Subsequently slaves also took over many of these positions. By the start of the eighteenth century there was little demand for indentured servants in the southern colonies, but they continued to be used elsewhere as skilled craftsmen, domestic servants, and even farm laborers.

There are conflicting accounts of the conditions faced by indentured servants. They reflect differences from place to place and master to master and the points of view of observers. A fairly positive account was given by George Alsop from Maryland in the middle of the seventeenth century:

"Then let such, where Providence hath ordained to live as Servants, either in England or beyond Sea, endure the prefixed yoak of their limited time with patience, and then in a small computation of years, by an industrious endeavour, they may become Masters and Mistresses of families themselves. And let this be spoke to the deserved praise of Mary-Land, That the four years I served there were not to me so slavish, as a two years Servitude of a Handicraft Apprenticeship was here in London."

Although many servants were better off than the poor in the slums of British cities, life for servants in the Americas was harsh. Long hours of hard labor were expected of people who were unaccustomed to fieldwork and regular employment. They were exposed to a different climate and new diseases. Not surprisingly many died before they completed their indentures, often within months of arriving in America. On the other hand, some completed their service and went on to achieve modest prosperity as free citizens. It is not known how many succeeded in this way, but historian Abbot Emerson Smith estimated only about one in ten was successful. A few returned to Europe, while many others became the impoverished citizens needing the poor relief that we will look at later in this book.

BELOW: **An engraving from the 1790s of a man sitting at a table being served by his maid. Indentured servants' conditions of service depended on their master's whim.**

Letter from an Indentured Servant

Richard Frethorne had the misfortune to be an indentured servant in the early decades of the Virginia colony.

At this time the colonists were still struggling to establish a workable system of food production and were under constant threat of attack from hostile Native Americans. Excerpts from his letter, written to his parents in 1623, provide a graphic account of the harsh conditions that claimed so many servants before their indenture period expired.

"LOVING AND KIND FATHER AND MOTHER:

My most humble duty remembered to you, hoping in god of your good health, as I myself am at the making hereof. This is to let you understand that I your child am in a most heavy case by reason of the country, [which] is such that it causeth much sickness, [such] as the scurvy and the bloody flux and diverse other diseases, which maketh the body very poor and weak. And when we are sick there is nothing to comfort us; for since I came out of the ship I never ate anything but peas, and loblollie (that is, water gruel). As for deer or venison I never saw any since I came into this land. There is indeed some fowl, but we are not allowed to go and get it, but must work hard both early and late for a mess of water gruel and a mouthful of bread and beef. A mouthful of bread for a penny loaf must serve for four men

which is most pitiful. [You would be grieved] if you did know as much as I [do], when people cry out day and night....For we live in fear of the enemy every hour, yet we have had a combat with them...and we took two alive and made slaves of them. But it was by policy, for we are in great danger; for our plantation is very weak by reason of the death and sickness of our company. For we came but twenty for the merchants, and they are half dead just; and we look every hour when two more should go. Yet there came some four other men yet to live with us, of which there is but one alive; and our Lieutenant is dead, and [also] his father and his brother. And there was some five or six of the last year's twenty, of which there is but three left, so that we are fain to get other men to plant with us; and yet we are but 32 to fight against 3000 if they should come. And the nighest help that we have is ten mile of us, and when the rogues overcame this place [the] last [time] they slew 80 persons. How then shall we do, for we lie even in their teeth?

"And I have nothing to comfort me, nor is there nothing to be gotten here but sickness and death, except [in the event] that one had money to lay out in some things for profit. But I have nothing at all no, not a shirt to my back but two rags

(2), nor clothes but one poor suit, nor but one pair of shoes, but one pair of stockings, but one cap, [and] but two bands [collars]. My cloak is stolen by one of my fellows, and to his dying hour [he] would not tell me what he did with it; but some of my fellows saw him have butter and beef out of a ship, which my cloak, I doubt [not], paid for. So that I have not a penny, nor a penny worth, to help me too either spice or sugar or strong waters, without the which one cannot live here....But I am not half [of] a quarter so strong as I was in England, and all is for want of victuals; for I do protest unto you that I have eaten more in [one] day at home than I have allowed me here for a week."

ABOVE: **A servant woman holds a steaming pot.**

RIGHT: **Servants were on call at all hours for all types of jobs—such as helping the mistress of the house put on her wig.**

27

Although eighteenth-century British law imposed the death penalty for all felonies—including many crimes that would now be regarded as minor—most criminals were not executed. Instead, many were sentenced to be sent to the colonies.

Soon a system of transportation contractors emerged. Wealthy merchants were granted contracts to transport all convicts at a fixed rate per head. In 1718 Jonathon Forward, one of the most active contractors, received £3 per person for felons taken from London's Newgate prison and £5 per person for those collected in the provinces. The contractor had to offer a bond for each prisoner that was forfeited if he or she returned to England. They also had to finance and arrange the prisoner's transportation to the Americas. Conditions on prison ships were even worse than those to which regular indentured servants were subjected. Often 10 percent or more died en route. Once in the colonies, the convicts were sold as indentured servants, gaining another £5 to £15 per head for the trader. The terms of their indenture were far longer than for normal servants—usually seven to fourteen years.

Despite the demand for labor, many colonists were not enthusiastic about serving as a dumping ground for criminals and murderers. Consider this commentary from the *Virginia Gazette*, May 25, 1751:

"When we see our Papers fill'd continually with accounts of the most audacious Robberies, the most Cruel Murders, and infinite other Villanies perpetrated by Convicts transported from Europe, what melancholy, what terrible Reflections must it occasion! What will become of our Posterity? These are some of thy Favours Britain. Thou art called our Mother Country; but what good Mother ever sent Thieves and Villains to accompany her children; to corrupt some with their infectious Vices and murder the rest? What Father ever endeavour'd to spread the Plague in his Family? We do not ask Fish, but thou gavest us Serpents, and more than Serpents! In what can Britain show a more Sovereign contempt for us than by emptying their jails into our settlements; unless they would likewise empty their Jakes [toilets] on our tables!"

Complaints like this alleging terrible crimes by transported convicts were regularly aired in the American press. Frequent attempts were made to outlaw the importation of convicts or to impose conditions on ship captains that would make it unprofitable. Generally the British Privy Council struck down these restrictions. Small numbers of convicts were taken to Caribbean colonies and to New Jersey and Pennsylvania, but the vast majority went to Maryland and Virginia, where the demand for plantation labor meant that they could be sold most profitably. One scholar estimated the total number arriving in those two colonies during the eighteenth century at a little more than 20,000. Of them about 80 percent were male. Not surprisingly many convicts were not reformed by their punishment and committed crimes such as assault, robbery, and prostitution in the colonies.

Prisoners and rebels

Far smaller numbers of prisoners were sent to the colonies after being captured in war. A few hundred mainly Scottish prisoners, captured from defeated Royalist armies late in the English Civil War, were sent to Virginia and Boston in 1654 and 1655. There they received relatively good treatment, and many are thought to have prospered as settlers after receiving their freedom. Larger numbers of Irish were also sent to the colonies after the English Civil War. They were either prisoners or "vagabonds" rounded up as a public nuisance in politically motivated sweeps during Puritan persecution of the Catholic rural population. In the 1660s a handful of unfortunate Quakers were sent to the New World, while about 800 rebel Scots were exiled between 1678 and 1685. Another batch of several hundred Scottish rebels were sent to the colonies after the Jacobite uprising of 1715, and a similar number followed in 1746.

BRIDEWELL PRISON

British prisons provided its colonies with many indentured servants and laborers. Bridewell is a good example. The first Bridewell Prison was built in 1515–1520 as a royal palace for Henry VIII. It was given to the City of London for the reception of vagrants and the punishment of petty offenders and disorderly women. It supplied numerous women prisoners who were transported to a life of servitude in the American colonies.

TOP AND ABOVE: Two views of Bridewell Prison, the upper by William Hogarth in 1732.

ABOVE LEFT: **At the end of the eighteenth century major American cities began to build appropriate facilities to deal with the criminals who had inevitably accompanied rapid urban growth. This illustration shows Walnut Street Jail in Philadelphia, Pennsylvania, in 1799.**

From the beginning of the eighteenth century the redemptioners system provided an alternative to indenture for poor people seeking to reach the Americas.

Starting in 1708, many German and Swiss migrants headed down the Rhine River to the port of Rotterdam, where they negotiated passage to the colonies for themselves and their families. Most had some money from selling their small plots of land and houses, but not enough to transport the whole family and their baggage. They paid what they could and on arrival in America had a short period, usually 14 days, to find the balance and "redeem" their debt. Usually they were unable to raise the money. As a result, some or all of the family would be sold as indentured servants for as long as necessary to raise the needed funds. After completing the service, they would rejoin the family group, mostly as farmers in Pennsylvania. Smaller numbers of Irish and British migrants also traveled under the same terms.

A German immigrant, Gottlieb Mittelberger, provided a riveting account of the redemptioner's voyage to life in the New World:

"The people are packed densely, like herrings so to say, in the large sea-vessels. One person receives a place of scarcely 2 feet width and 6 feet length in the bedstead, while many a ship carries four to six hundred souls....For from there the ships, unless they have good wind, must often sail 8, 9, 10 to 12 weeks before they reach Philadelphia. But even with the best wind the voyage lasts 7 weeks.

TOP: **Rotterdam, the exit point for many of the redemptioners fleeing poverty in Germany and Switzerland, seen in an engraving from around 1700.**

ABOVE: **Philadelphia is where many redemptioners arrived and sought to find someone to redeem their debt. If they could not settle what they owed, they would have to enter service for as long as was needed to pay off their debts.**

"But during the voyage there is on board these ships terrible misery, stench, fumes, horror, vomiting, many kinds of sea-sickness, fever, dysentery, headache, heat, constipation, boils, scurvy, cancer, mouth rot, and the like, all of which come from old and sharply salted food and meat, also from very bad and foul water, so that many die miserably.

"Add to this want of provisions, hunger, thirst, frost, heat, dampness, anxiety, want, afflictions and lamentations, together with other trouble....The misery reaches the climax when a gale rages for 2 or 3 nights and days, so that every one believes that the ship will go to the bottom with all human beings on board. In such a visitation the people cry and pray most piteously. Children from 1 to 7 years rarely survive the voyage.

"When the ships have landed at Philadelphia after their long voyage, no one is permitted to leave them except those who pay for their passage or can give good security; the others, who cannot pay, must remain on board the ships till they are purchased, and are released from the ships by their purchasers. The sick always fare the worst, for the healthy are naturally preferred and purchased first; and so the sick and wretched must often remain on board in front of the city for 2 or 3 weeks, and frequently die, whereas many a one, if he could pay his debt and were permitted to leave the ship immediately, might recover and remain alive.

"The sale of human beings in the market on board the ship is carried out thus: Every day Englishmen, Dutchmen and High-German people come from the city of Philadelphia and other places, in part from a great distance, say 20,

30, or 40 hours away, and go on board the newly arrived ship that has brought and offers for sale passengers from Europe, and select among the healthy persons such as they deem suitable for their business, and bargain with them how long they will serve for their passage money, which most of them are still in debt for. When they have come to an agreement, it happens that adult persons bind themselves in writing to serve 3, 4, 5 or 6 years for the amount due by them, according to their age and strength.

ABOVE: **Amish farmer Daniel Stoltzfus drags a wheelbarrow through one of his barns in Wakefield, Pennsylvania. The Amish, traditionalist farmers who spurn machinery and other modern conveniences, live off the land much as they have for centuries in communities spread across the Midwest and East in rural America. They give a glimpse into what life must have been like two centuries ago.**

But very young people, from 10 to 15 years, must serve till they are 21 years old."

The first Africans arrived in Virginia and the other colonies within a few years of their founding. In 1650 there were 400 Africans in Virginia out of a total population of about 19,000.

At that time their legal status was uncertain, and most were indentured servants working alongside white immigrants. "Freedom dues" of a small plot of land and supplies were usually given to them once their service was completed. Already a change was under way establishing a system of racially based slavery. In 1641 Massachusetts became the first colony to legally recognize slavery. Over the second half of the seventeenth century the English colonies in North America passed acts that redefined the legal status of black people as slaves and restricted their involvement with whites. The following is from a law passed in Maryland:

> "Bee it Enacted…That all Negroes or other slaves already within the Province And all Negroes and other slaves to bee hereafter imported into the Province shall serve DuranteVita [service for life]. And all Children born of any Negroe or other slave shall be Slaves as their fathers were for the term of their lives.
>
> "Bee it further Enacted…That whatsoever freeborne woman shall intermarry with any slave from and after the last day of this present Assembly shall Serve the master of such slave during the life of her husband And that all the issue [children] of such freeborne women so married shall be Slaves as their fathers were."

Reverend Peter Fontaine was more troubled by moral anxieties than was

ABOVE: **A train of chained slaves was called a "coffle." Here a coffle passes by the U.S. Capitol in Washington, D.C., around 1820.**

BELOW LEFT: **A slave auction. Slaves were the most underprivileged of all members of American society. Without any rights, they were seen in law as their owner's goods.**

THE ABOLITION MOVEMENT

The abolition movement grew stronger in the nineteenth century and started a debate. Were slaves better off than the free white poor either in the North or in European cities? It was true that slaves could usually expect to be provided at least with the minimum necessary for survival; masters were unlikely to starve their own property to death. Proslavery writers in the South, such as George Fitzhugh, made fanciful claims that slaves lived a life of comfort and security:

> "The negro slaves of the South are the happiest, and, in some sense, the freest people in the world. The children and the aged and infirm work not at all, and yet have all the comforts and necessaries of life provided for them."

typical of slave owners, but his 1757 letter to his brother summarizes the southern planter's economic motivation for owning slaves:

"Before our troubles, you could not hire a servant or slave for love or money, so that, unless robust enough to cut wood, to go to mill, to work at the hoe, etc., you must starve or board in some family where they both fleece and half starve you. There is no set price upon corn, wheat, and provisions; so they take advantage of the necessities of strangers, who are thus obliged to purchase some slaves and land. This, of course, draws us all into the original sin and curse of the country of

purchasing slaves, and this is the reason we have no merchants, traders, or artificers of any sort but what become planters in a short time."

The poorest Americans

Slaves were in many ways the least privileged and poorest people in early America. Their legal status was as property or goods rather than as persons. In law they had no rights. They were not protected from arbitrary treatment, were subject to a wide range of barbaric punishments, and in the eyes of the law could own no possessions. Each slave's situation varied depending on how long they had been in the colony, their age, their abilities, and the economic roles they

filled. In addition their status was greatly affected by their master's circumstances and personality.

Newly arrived Africans stripped of their possessions, families, language, and culture had no resources except their own heritage and mental and physical strength to sustain them. Over time Africans adapted to their lives as slaves and reestablished ties to others. They found a role in which they worked and lived and—if possible—remade a family. Slaves born in the Americas grew up in slavery and came to understand its rules and conventions. They adopted various roles in the plantation household or fields as required. Older slaves who showed special ability were promoted to supervisory positions or trained as skilled craftsmen. They usually received

modest extra privileges for themselves and their family in return.

This quotation from an ex-slave, Reverand Josiah Henson (who became the inspiration for Harriet Beecher Stowe's classic antislavery novel *Uncle Tom's Cabin*), describes the conditions under which they lived:

"My earliest employments were, to carry buckets of water to the men at work, and to hold a horse-plough, used for weeding between the rows of corn. As I grew older and taller, I was entrusted with the care of master's saddle-horse. Then a hoe was put into my hands, and I was soon required to do the day's work of a man; and it was not long before I could do it, at least as well as my associates in misery.

"…The principal food of those upon my master's plantation consisted of corn-meal and salt herrings; to which was added in summer a little buttermilk, and the few vegetables which each might raise for himself and his family, on the little piece of ground which was assigned to him for the purpose, called a truck-patch.

"In ordinary times we had two regular meals in a day: breakfast at twelve o'clock, after laboring from daylight, and supper when the work of the remainder of the day was over. In harvest season we had three. Our dress was of tow-cloth; for the children, nothing but a shirt; for the older ones a pair of pantaloons or a gown in addition, according to the sex. Besides these, in the winter a round jacket or overcoat, a wool-hat once in two or three years, for the males, and a pair of coarse shoes once a year.

"We lodged in log huts, and on the bare ground. Wooden floors were an unknown luxury. In a single room were huddled, like cattle, ten or a dozen persons, men, women, and children. All ideas of refinement and decency were, of course, out of the question. We had neither bedsteads, nor furniture of any description. Our beds were collections of straw and old rags, thrown down in the corners and boxed in with boards; a single blanket the only covering. Our favorite way of sleeping, however, was on a plank, our heads raised on an old jacket and our feet toasting before the smoldering fire. The wind whistled and the rain and snow blew in through the cracks, and the damp earth soaked in the moisture till the floor was miry as a pig-sty. Such were our houses. In these

wretched hovels were we penned at night, and fed by day; here were the children born and the sick neglected."

A master might—and frequently did—choose to beat one of his slaves to death. Frederick Douglass, who spent his early life as a slave, became one of the most forceful advocates for abolition. In his now celebrated 1852 speech entitled "The Meaning of July Fourth for the Negro" he asked:

"What, am I to argue that it is wrong to make men brutes, to rob them of their liberty, to work them without wages, to keep them ignorant of their relations to their fellow men, to beat them with sticks, to flay their flesh with the lash, to load their limbs with irons, to hunt them with dogs, to sell them

at auction, to sunder their families, to knock out their teeth, to burn their flesh, to starve them into obedience and submission to their masters?"

In early America slaves suffered the ultimate lack of security. Everything they had, including their own family, was dependent on the whims of the master and could be taken from them at any time without notice. Some free black men and women managed to establish a reasonable life for themselves as skilled workers, craftsmen, tenant farmers, or even small landowners on the fringes of colonial society. Most, however, were trapped alongside poor whites at the lowest levels of society, as Douglass put it in his autobiography, "kept upon the narrowest margin between life and starvation." There they suffered racial discrimination, the insecurity of their

ABOVE AND ABOVE LEFT: **Two impressions of the conditions under which the slavers operated. In fact, even though the artists have tried to show suffering, these romanticized images cannot convey the true horrror of the journey. Slaves had far less space than shown here. They were wedged together on narrow shelves stacked in very low holds that were often flooded with polluted water. Large numbers died before they even reached America. For more information on slave ships go to the fourth volume in this set: Transporters.**

uncertain legal status, and the pressures of life on the edge of poverty. When they were forced by hardship to apply for poor relief, they were less likely to be helped—and for shorter periods—than their white neighbors.

Phillis Wheatley

The eighteenth-century slave Phillis Wheatley became one of America's best-loved poets. She was born on the western coast of Africa, probably in Senegal, in about 1753. She was kidnapped by slave traders at about eight years of age and transported to America.

P O E M S

ON

VARIOUS SUBJECTS,

RELIGIOUS AND MORAL.

BY

PHILLIS WHEATLEY,

NEGRO SERVANT to Mr. JOHN WHEATLEY,
of BOSTON, in NEW ENGLAND.

LONDON:

Printed for A. BELL, Bookseller, Aldgate; and sold by
Meſſrs. COX and BERRY, King-Street, BOSTON.

M DCC LXXIII.

Publiſhed according to Act of Parliament, Sept. 1, 1773 by Archd. Bell,
Bookſeller No. 8 near the Saracens Head Aldgate.

Phillis was taken to Boston and bought by a tailor, John Wheatley, as a maid for his wife. Her original name, Fatou, was replaced with that of her master. The Wheatleys decided to provide their young slave with a rudimentary edu-cation and began to teach her to read and write. To their surprise, within 16 months of her arrival in America she was proficient in English, Greek, and Latin, as well as history, geography, and astronomy. Her first poem was published in the *Newport and Rhode Island Mercury* on December 21, 1767.

In spite of this initial success, Phillis could not find a Boston publisher who would consider her work. Eventually she and the Wheatleys were forced to look across the Atlantic for a publisher. After a trip to London her first volume was published in 1773. This was her only book to be published during her lifetime. The collection, called *Poems on Various Subjects, Religious and Moral*, contained 39 original poems by Phyllis. It has a place in history as the first poetry published by an African American.

Soon after their return from England the Wheatleys gave Phillis her freedom, and she married a free black man, John Peters. Sadly this marriage was dissolved after Peters abandoned her. Phillis subsequently took a job as a servant, and she died in poverty in 1784.

Although Wheatley was a vocal critic of slavery, she was limited by the poetic forms of the eighteenth century. The difference between her poetry and the anger of her many letters and private notes is striking. In "On Being Brought from Africa to America" Wheatley makes her only poetic reference to her position as a slave:

'Twas mercy brought me from my pagan land, Taught my benighted soul to understand That there's a God, that there's a Saviour too: Once I redemption neither sought nor knew. Some view our race with scornful eye: 'Their colour is a diabolic dye.' Remember Christians, negroes black as Cain May be refined and join th' angelic train."

Now compare the poem to this letter Wheatley wrote to Reverend Samson Occum in which she passionately argues against slavery:

"I have this Day received your obliging kind Epistle, and am greatly satisfied with your Reasons respecting the Negroes, and think highly reasonable what you offer in Vindication of their natural Rights: Those that invade them cannot be insensible that the divine Light is chasing away the thick Darkness which broods over the Land of Africa; and the Chaos which has reign'd so long, is converting into beautiful Order, and [r]eveals more and more clearly, the glorious Dispensation of civil and religious Liberty, which are so inseparably Limited, that there is little or no Enjoyment of one Without the other: Otherwise, perhaps, the Israelites had been less solicitous for their Freedom from Egyptian slavery; I do not say they would have been contented without it, by no means, for in every human Breast, God has implanted a Principle, which we call Love of Freedom; it is impatient of Oppression, and pants for Deliverance; and by the Leave of our modern Egyptians I will assert, that the same Principle lives in us. God grant Deliverance in his own Way and Time, and get him honour upon all those whose Avarice impels them to countenance and help forward tile Calamities of their fellow Creatures. This I desire not for their Hurt, but to convince them of the strange Absurdity of their Conduct whose Words and Actions are so diametrically, opposite. How well the Cry for Liberty, and the reverse Disposition for the exercise of oppressive Power over others agree, I humbly think it does not require the Penetration of a Philosopher to determine."

In the 1700s New York, Boston, Philadelphia, Charleston, and Newport rapidly grew to become urban centers comparable to the leading cities of Europe. Although conditions were never as bad as in the slums of Europe, city leaders were faced with many problems caused by a growing number of poor people.

The cost of caring for the poor was the main expense for city budgets, and it continued to rise. Yet the existing system of poor relief was not able to deal with the problem. Colonial cities and towns had to find ways to deal with growing number of penniless widows, abandoned wives, crippled working men, the mentally ill, chronic alcoholics, unemployed sailors, and orphaned children. Consider this report from the *New York Journal* in 1737:

"I believe it would be a very shocking Appearance to a moralized Heathen, were he to meet with an Object in Human Shape, half starved with Cold, with Clothes out at the Elbows, Knees through the Breeches, Hair standing on end, Commanding the Almighty to Curse, Damn, Stink, Rot, etc. all and every Thing that seems to offend....Yet this is what we must see and hear every Day with Impunity, even from Children scarce able to utter their Words. From the age of about four to fourteen they spend their Days in the Streets, with Marvels, Tops, Hoops, Farthings, etc.—then they are put out as Apprentices, perhaps for four, five, or six Years, so they too often become their own Masters before they know what it is to obey."

In response to the growing problem the decades before the Revolution were a period of changing ideas and approach-es. New beliefs about the causes of poverty took hold, and new institutions were introduced to deal with the problem. As a result the poor-relief system that had earlier seemed effective was gradually changed.

The poor-relief system

The poor in Colonial America had a customary and a legal right to help from the public authorities. This should have protected them from hunger and homelessness at times when they were unable to fend for themselves. Poor relief followed the model established in England, which was based on the Elizabethan Poor Law of 1601. At its heart were three components. The first was "out relief," under which city officials would authorize and hand out small payments to meet the immediate needs of poor people. Those who were homeless were lodged with a willing

member of the community, ideally a relative or friend. The "host" was paid an agreed amount per week for the cost of housing and food. The names of both aid recipients and those contracted to assist them were usually carefully set down in town records by the poor-relief officials, although generally nothing else is known of either party. For example, in 1663 Edward Weeddine was paid £6 by Boston town officials to provide one year's food and lodging for Elizabeth Ward. Whenever possible, recipients were expected to do some kind of work in return for the aid.

The second component of poor relief was using apprenticeships or service contracts to deal with orphans and the children of the poor. Mothers or families with infants usually received aid together. But once children reached age five to seven, they were usually taken away from their mother and placed with another, richer household. There they became a domestic servant or apprentice under a contract that lasted until they became adults. Usually the contract required that the child receive a basic education at the expense of the new master. An incident recorded in almshouse records in 1800 illustrates a typical circumstance in which a child might come to the attention of poor-relief officials and be subject to an apprenticeship contract:

> "When a constable picked up eight year old William Thomas for begging in the street, the boy explained that while his father 'had been gone to sea' his mother 'goes out washing of cloaths [clothes]' for a livelihood [and] leaves him at home to take care of his Brother. When his brother cried out from hunger, William went soliciting bread."

Sadly no record was kept of what either William or his parents thought of the treatment he received.

The final component of colonial poor relief was the practice known as "warning out." Out relief was financed by taxes on townspeople. Towns were always on the lookout to ensure that aid was given only to those people they felt were entitled to receive it. This entitlement was established not just on the basis of whether they were in genuine need. To qualify for relief, a person also had to be a legal resident of that place. Legal residence in a town was obtained by birth, by completing a full term of servitude in the town, or by purchasing land. Simply living in a town—no matter for how long—was not enough to make someone a legal resident.

People who needed relief but were not residents or new arrivals in a town who could not show means of supporting themselves were "warned out." That

ABOVE: **Scenes of immoral behavior and drunkenness in London's "Gin Lane and Beer Street," about 1751. Although poverty and overcrowding in the new American cities never reached the levels seen in London, city officials became increasingly concerned by the damaging side effects of urban growth.**

meant they were told to leave immediately and were punished, often with 30 lashes of the whip, if they

returned. Strangers were often required to post a bond (a deposit of money with authorities) before being permitted to remain in a town. This policy could often be harsh and even arbitrary. In the case described below, a woman who is about to give birth—and has not even asked for relief—was forced to leave the town of Chelmsford, Massachusetts, so that any costs might be met by her husband:

"The Select men having sent for John Plum and his daughter Mercy, and finding that his said daughter being married to Thomas Chub of Beurlee, and being also near the

time of her delivery is not provided for by her said husband, nor taken to home to him, but continues here with her father, contrary to good order, and to hazarding of a charge upon the town, do therefore order and require, that the said Mercy Chub do speedily within Six or eight days leave this towne, and betake herself to her said husband. And do also warn and order the said John Plum that he no longer entertain his said daughter, but hasten to her husband as aforesaid upon the penalty by the town order in that Case provided."

Warning out the poor worked well in small villages where everyone knew each other and the details of their neighbors' lives. But this practice became more difficult to maintain when towns grew larger. In the major cities monitoring the poor was a serious challenge. In Boston the town officers, known as selectmen, found that administering poor relief took up much of their time. As a result in 1691 they appointed four men as "overseers of the poor." The number of overseers was increased to eight in 1706.

A community response

Poor relief was a community enterprise involving most of the population in the affairs of needy citizens. People were either involved directly, by caring for a destitute neighbor, or they were involved indirectly by paying taxes, which were usually unpopular. People also believed that it was a moral and religious duty to take responsibility for the less fortunate. Town officials used a direct, face-to-face approach for giving aid. They based their decisions on personal knowledge of the people's circumstances and on information gathered from others. Because aid was generally given for only short periods, the same people might appear before them again and again.

Wherever possible, officials would urge a claimant's family, friends, neighbors, or church to help the person. If no aid was available from those places, the town might first try to help by giving the person a tax credit or free firewood. Only as a last resort did they commit money. Usually they gave as little as possible for as short a time as possible. Recipients were encouraged to work in return for the money and were closely monitored. Overseers of the poor worked closely with their counterparts in nearby towns to decide who was responsible for each person. They tried to reclaim the costs of helping a resident of another town or to balance those costs against aid given to

THE GROWING POWER OF THE STATE

Over the course of the eighteenth century the largest colonial towns in America—including Boston, New York, Philadelphia, and Charleston—became rapidly expanding cities. As their populations increased, the costs of providing for the poor rose, leading to resentment and division, as we shall see in the next section.

Top: The Old State House—better known as Independence Hall—in Philadelphia. This famous building served as the meeting place of the Second Continental Congress and was the site of the signing of the Declaration of Independence and the drafting of the U.S. Constitution.

Above: The Maryland State House, where the Annapolis Convention took place in 1786. Representatives from five states (Delaware, New Jersey, New York, Pennsylvania, and Virginia) produced a report that called for a meeting of all states the following year in Philadelphia—the Constitutional Convention.

one of their own residents elsewhere. Population growth in the eighteenth century made this personalized system of poor relief very expensive. And even with the money spent, communities found they were not solving the problems caused by growing numbers of poor people.

In Boston the annual cost of supporting the poor rose from £800 in 1727 to £4,000 in 1737. Similarly dramatic and much resented increases occurred in Philadelphia, New York, and in towns both large and small.

Cities tried harsh restrictions on newcomers, including requiring ship captains to post bonds (deposit a sum of money as a guarantee) for new arrivals. But growing immigration and rising numbers of penniless residents put the poor-relief system under strain.

As the century went on, the moral climate also changed. Earlier, people had seen status in life as ordained by God. They regarded it as a blessing to have the opportunity to help those God had placed in positions of need. By the 1750s more people regarded their own success as won by hard work and pious living. It seemed to follow that those who were poor might also be in their situation through their own laziness and moral failings. Greater distinction, it was argued, must be drawn between the "deserving" poor and the "undeserving" poor. The "deserving" poor were people such as abandoned mothers, orphans, and those afflicted by illness or serious injury who were suitable for aid. The "undeserving" were mainly able-bodied men and women who were unable to find employment.

Today we might argue that forces beyond the control of poor people caused unemployment. We understand that factors such as seasonal patterns of agriculture and shipping, and the balance of trade between the American colonies and England, affected how many jobs were available. But in the eyes of some eighteenth-century citizens people who did not work were simply lazy or drunkards. It was thought they had failed to take advantage of the opportunities open to anyone willing to work hard and live modestly. It was argued that these undeserving poor should be reformed and taught a morally correct way of living. Many felt that new forms of aid were needed, and more supervision was required, to better meet the needs of both the deserving and the undeserving poor.

Changing attitudes were demonstrated in a Virginia law of 1755 that required recipients of poor relief to identify themselves. The law said that they:

"Shall, upon the shoulder of the right sleeve of his or her upper most garment, in an open and visible manner, wear a badge, with the name of the parish to which he or she belongs, cut either in blue, red, or green cloth."

Failure to display this badge was punishable by loss of relief or even by a public whipping. This extreme measure was a response to the changing climate of opinions that also prompted creation of new institutions such as almshouses, workhouses, and hospitals for the poor.

Small and poorly funded almshouses (also known as poorhouses) had existed in a few communities since the early eighteenth century. They were used as an alternative, or a backup, to the

ABOVE: **Blackwell's Island, New York, was known for its workhouse, its penitentiary, and its almshouses, for men and women, erected in the first half of the nineteenth century (illustrated here).**

RIGHT: **Blockley Almshouse was located on the west side of the Schuylkill River opposite Philadelphia. The establishment housed an average of more than 1,800 poor people each year.**

standard "outdoor" relief system. The Quakers built and financed the first almshouse in Philadelphia in 1717. In the second half of the 1700s the number and size of these institutions increased greatly. Soon the balance of aid was shifted toward more reliance on so-called "indoor" relief. Almshouses, where the "deserving" poor were helped, were supposed to be very different from the workhouses where the "undeserving" were forced to reform their ways. The following quotation from the *Pennsylvania Gazette* of May 29, 1760, provides a good guide to attitudes expressed toward those who were considered "worthy" of charity:

"In a City of large Trade, many poorer People must be employed in carrying on a Commerce, which subjects them to frequent terrible Accidents—That in a Country where great Numbers of indigent Foreigners have been but lately imported, and where the common Distresses of Poverty have been much increased, by a most savage and bloody War, there must be many Poor, there must be many sick and Maimed—That poor People are maintained by their Labor, and, if they cannot labor, they cannot live without the Help of the more Fortunate—We all know many Mouths are fed, many Bodies clothed by one poor Man's Diligence and Industry; should any distemper seize and afflict this Person; should any sudden Hurt happen to him, which should render him incapable to follow the business of his Calling, unfit him to work, disable him to labor, even but for a little Time; or should his Duty to aged and diseased Parents, or his fatherly Tenderness for an afflicted Child, engross his Attention and Care, how great must be the Calamity of such a Family! How pressing their wants!"

Traditional outdoor relief continued alongside the greater reliance on almshouses. The mix varied according the needs of individual cases and the preferences of the officials involved. Aid recipients were sometimes able to change the forms of aid they were given. Often they appealed to overseers or asked a respectable friend or relative to speak on their behalf. Other times they refused to cooperate with the almshouse wardens or even ran away. Many of those sent to the almshouses were young mothers with infants, elderly men, women with no surviving family, and those too ill or disabled to work. Conditions varied with the wealth of the community and the quality of the overseers. Generally all residents received at least basic housing, food, and medical attention. In return those who were capable were expected to work within the institution to contribute to their upkeep. Most people were not long-term residents of almshouses. They were permitted to stay only as long as they were in need and were sent away as soon as possible. Unfortunately many soon returned. Often people entered an almshouse during harsh winters and left in the spring when the temperatures rose, and opportunities for casual work increased.

The undeserving poor?

In theory there was a sharp distinction made between almshouses and workhouses. Workhouses focused on the moral reform of the supposedly unworthy poor and the able-bodied but unemployed. Because of this they offered a very strict lifestyle. This extract from the bylaws of Chelmsford workhouse conveys the intentions of the firm system that was typical:

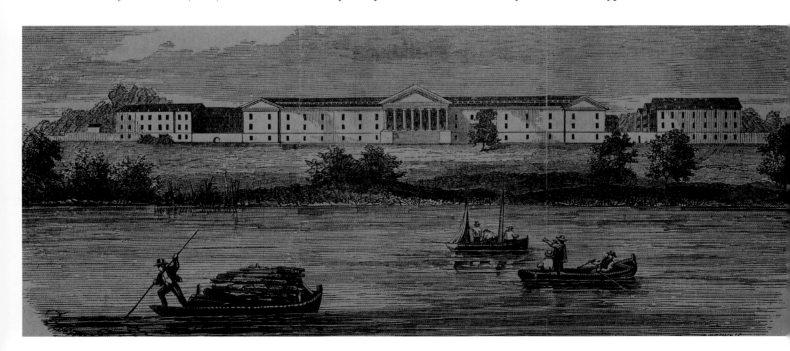

"7. The master of the workhouse shall have power to reward the faithful and industrious by granting favors and...to punish at his discretion the idle, stubborn, disorderly and disobedient by immediate confinement without any food other than bread and water.

"8. The master of the workhouse shall cause said house and furniture to be kept clean and in good order, and shall cause habits of cleanliness, neatness and decency to be strictly observed by all persons received into said workhouse.

"9. The master of the workhouse shall cause the Lord's Day to be strictly observed.

"10. Every person who may be received into said workhouse or be a member thereof must obey the orders and regulations thereof and the commands of the master, and will be required by him diligently to work and labor as he shall direct, according to age, health and capacity.

"11. Every person who shall absent himself from the said workhouse...shall be deemed to be an idle, stubborn and disorderly person, and punished accordingly.

"12. The use of spiritous liquors [alcohol] is strictly prohibited except when the master, physician or overseers of the workhouse shall otherwise order; and no person shall be allowed to have or keep in their possession or bring or receive any spiritous liquors into said workhouse."

Later (pages 46–47) we will look more closely at one such workhouse, the aptly named "Bettering House" in Philadelphia. This case study will show that often the reform and lifestyle changes supposedly encouraged by these institutions were, in fact, rarely achieved.

Today we recognize the differences between charitable institutions like almshouses and places for the sick such as hospitals and asylums. But in the eighteenth century these distinctions were only starting to emerge. The mentally ill were placed with any citizens ready to care for them in their home. Often a kind of reverse auction was used to establish the lowest cost to public funds. Women in the home routinely provided most medical care, assisted by trained doctors or local clergymen with medical experience. Many of these doctors voluntarily provided assistance to some of those who were too poor to pay them. City poor-relief funds often included an annual payment to a doctor who was able to treat the poor, either in their home or at the almshouse.

Poverty and health care

By midcentury people began to realize that almshouses were not the best places to care for the sick or the mentally ill. Neither the healthy nor the ill were seen as benefiting from living together. The simple facilities and weak knowledge of sanitation made them dangerous sources of infection. However, there were few facilities to care for the sick that were too poor to be cared for in their own homes. One exception was the Pennsylvania Hospital for the Sick Poor. It was established Philadelphia in 1751 by prominent Quaker businessmen at the urging of Benjamin Franklin. He argued that a strict lifestyle and more effective care would speed the return of sick workers to their employers. This, he

PENNSYLVANIA HOSPITAL

The Pennsylvania Hospital for the Sick Poor, founded in 1751 in Philadelphia, was the first general hospital in America. Benjamin Franklin was instrumental in raising money to build the hospital. Pennsylvania Hospital was initially concerned with returning poor people to health so that they could get back to work and support their families. Bad hygiene and lack of medical knowledge made hospitals dangerous places—avoided by any who could afford home treatment.

harshly treated and resentful of the officials and the wealthy charity providers? No letters or dairies from relief recipients survive to provide any direct account of their views and voices, but poor-relief records are full of brief references to complaints and arguments indicating that the poor challenged and disputed aspects of their treatment. A brief remark attributed to a Philadelphia laborer with a large family by a newspaper is an extremely rare exception. The unnamed man complained that his earnings, however hard he tried, were insufficient to keep his family from the almshouse:

> "I have strove all in my power and find that I cannot support them."

He did not feel his poverty was justified or due to laziness. Deprived of the direct voices of poor-relief recipients, historians have studied what they can about the way they behaved as recorded in the poorhouse logbooks. There is evidence that many poor people developed strategies that frustrated attempts to control and "reform" them. They took what they could from aid when they needed it but tried to evade any of the controls that went with it. This complaint by New York city fathers in 1738 records a typical example:

> "Whereas several of the poor who are relieved in the poorhouse as objects of charity have of late (when well cloathed at the public charge) made a practice of absenting themselves from the said poorhouse and selling or making away with their clothing in the summertime and returning to the said poorhouse on the approaching winter almost naked, to the great expense and charge of the parish, for their clothing to defend them from the inclemency of the weather and preserve them from perishing by cold."

felt, would reduce the cost to the public of supporting them and their families. Even in this case, however, it was clear that ideas about the proper role of the poor were more important than concern for treating the sick. Slowly more facilities to treat the real medical needs of the poor started to appear. A hospital

for the mentally ill was established in Williamsburg in 1773, and a poor hospital was opened in New York in 1791.

What did the recipients of poor relief think of the assistance they were subjected to? Were they just grateful for what they were given and happy to do as they were told in return, or did they feel

The Bettering House

Benjamin Franklin was a key figure in building a new kind of almshouse in Philadelphia in the 1760s. This new house was built to demonstrate the latest progressive ideas about reforming the poor through hard work under private sponsorship, rather than at public expense.

Its name, the Bettering House, expressed its founders' belief that self-improvement was the solution to poverty. They believed that the poor should be supervised and motivated to change their ways that had caused them to be on public assistance. Then their failings such as laziness, low morals, and drunkenness would be replaced by

Christian virtues of hard work, thriftiness, and determination.

Franklin and other leading Quaker taxpayers were upset by the growing cost of poor relief. They were also inspired by what they regarded as the successful example of the earlier Hospital for the Sick Poor. In response they formed a group called the Contributors to the

Relief and Employment of the Poor of the City of Philadelphia, Southwark, Moyamensing, Passyunk, and the Northern Liberties. This group petitioned the Assembly to build a new and larger poorhouse with stricter and more effective supervision of the poor. The Bettering House was a huge structure with two wings and was located west of

Tenth Street. One wing was an alms-house for the infirm, nursing mothers, and deserving families in distress. The other wing was a work-house in which able-bodied people lived but were made to perform regular labor.

When the Bettering House opened in October 1767, it took in 284 residents. They were put to work at various tasks that would contribute toward their upkeep as well as reform their view of working. These jobs included making nails, picking oakum (unraveling lengths of old rope for reuse), and weaving cloth. Ministers regularly preached sermons to the inmates about improving their lives. Strict rules forbade idleness and the consumption of alcohol. The overseers, under the management of the contrib-utors, made every effort to teach what were called the "habits of industry."

The failure of reform

However, it was soon realized that the new institution was not achieving the success that had been expected. The building and its upkeep cost far more than could be raised from private sponsorship and the work done by inmates. As a result the hoped for cost savings from grouping many poor people in one building failed to materialize. The Bettering House continued to be a burden on taxpayers, and just as many poor people in Philadelphia asked for help as before.

Even worse, the Bettering House was not able to "reform" people as was hoped. Because inmates stayed in contact with their friends and families elsewhere in the city, it was impossible to strictly supervise them and maintain the "improving" system the founders had planned. Inmates sent away as reformed, hard-working Christians often returned when they couldn't find jobs. Plus the inmates often had their own ideas about being "reformed." Sometimes they refus-ed to work. Other times they ran away if the supervisors put too much pressure

on them, or they found better prospects elsewhere.

The Bettering House founders and other advocates of a new approach to poor relief learned an important lesson. They had failed to look at the entire world in which the poor lived. Poor people were at the mercy of events far outside their control. These events, rather than personal failings, often determined the opportunities open to them. Philadelphia in the 1760s faced a flood of refugees from frontier areas who had been displaced by the French and Indian War and Pontiac's Rebellion. These new poor people were clearly a bigger burden on the poor relief than those impoverished due to laziness or low morals.

ABOVE: **A poor family is shown living in a one-room home. Their daily lives would be consumed by the hard work of just staying alive, including doing the laundry, as seen here.**

LEFT: **The Bettering House on Spruce Street, Philadelphia, Pennsylvania, in 1799. The new almshouses built in the eighteenth century were frequently the largest buildings in each town, and much of the population was involved in supplying food and services for the inmates.**

Religion played a central role in the daily life of many early settlers in America. People escaping religious persecution established colonies in Pennsylvania and Massachusetts, and many colonists originally came to the New World seeking religious freedom.

Religious beliefs had a major impact on the treatment of the poor in all of the colonies, but especially so in Pennsylvania and Massachusetts. Both the Quakers (also known as the Society of Friends) and the Puritans felt that differences in status and circumstances in life were ordained by God. They also believed that it was the obligation of the faithful to do good by assisting those who were less favorably placed. Leading figures in Quaker Pennsylvania performed many personal acts of charity. They were instrumental in establishing almshouses and the Hospital for the Sick Poor. The Society of Friends tried to help both Quakers and members of other faiths who had fallen into hardship rather than leaving them to public relief. Starting in 1702, when they were left a small house on Walnut Street, Philadelphia, for housing the poor, the Quakers maintained an almshouse where whole families could be boarded.

The respected Puritan minister and writer Cotton Mather (1663-1728) offered humanitarian viewpoints that were far ahead of his time. He had great influence over the people of Massachusetts and encouraged them to help those in need in one of his most famous works:

ABOVE: *An Introduction to the Singing of Psalm Tunes*, written by the Reverend Tufts and published in Boston in 1721.

LEFT: **The Mother Bethel African Methodist Episcopal Church was the first U.S. church for an African American congregation. It was founded by Richard Allen in Philadelphia, Pennsylvania, in 1786.**

"Neighbors—be concerned that the orphans and widows in your neighborhood may be well provided for….While their next relatives were yet living, they were, perhaps, but meanly provided for. What must they now be in their more solitary condition? Their condition should be considered, and the result of the consideration be: 'I delivered the orphan that had no helper, and I caused the heart of the widow to sing for joy.' By consequence, all the afflicted in the neighborhood are to be thought upon. Sirs, it would be too much for you at least once in a week to think: 'What neighbor is reduced to pinching and painful poverty? Or in any degree impoverished with heavy losses?' Think: 'What neighbor is heartbroken with sad bereavements, bereaved of desirable relatives?' And think: 'What neighbor has a soul buffeted and hurried with violent assaults of the wicked one?' But then think: 'What shall be done for such neighbors?'…Give them all the assistances that may answer their occasions. Assist them with advice to them, assist them with address to others for them. And if it be needful, bestow your alms upon them."

Churches often took special collections to meet emergency needs. They collected money to support widows and orphans after a smallpox outbreak or to help families left on relief when soldiers were sent away to fight the French or Native Americans. In 1718, following a period of fighting with the French, Cotton Mather noted that "The Widows of the Flock are numerous, they make about a fifth Part of our Communicants." In 1741 a severe winter caused great suffering among the poor, and church collections in Boston on two Sundays raised the huge sum of £1,240 for emergency assistance. In New York the Dutch Reformed Church ran an almshouse for its poor members on Wall Street starting in 1701.

Poor relief in the South

In the southern colonies, such as Virginia, there were fewer feelings of religious obligation toward the poor. Landowners who saw themselves as English nobility felt a duty to help the impoverished. Interestingly, churches had an important role in managing this aid. Virginia was a crown colony (under direct control of the British government) and followed the English pattern of assigning poor relief to church parishes rather than towns or villages.

Each parish appointed 12 leaders, called vestrymen, whose principal duties were to collect tithes (payments used to support a church) and administer poor relief. The poor were usually first helped on an out relief basis. Families that agreed to take in boarders were often repaid with tobacco. Most parish funds were used to help widows, the sick, ex-indentured servants who had been unable to establish a livelihood, and abandoned or orphaned children. Children were placed with landowners as indentured servants, providing them with an important source of unpaid labor.

For the "deserving poor" the vestrymen in Charleston built an almshouse in 1734. By 1738 they had also built a larger workhouse and a hospital. Soon most of the poor in Charleston on out relief had been transferred to one of these institutions. By the middle of the eighteenth century the southern colonies experienced serious problems caring for war refugees, displaced Acadians, and other newly poor people. Finally, in the 1750s town and village authorities in Virginia and South Carolina began to assume a greater share of the growing burden of poor relief from the parishes.

MISSIONARY WORK

English Presbyterian missionary John Eliot addresses a gathering of Algonquins in 1660. Known as "the Apostle of the Indians," Eliot established the first church for Native Americans in Massachusetts.

Death and Burials

In the seventeenth and eighteenth centuries death was a constant factor. It affected life in a way that is hard to understand in today's developed countries. Life expectancy was extremely low.

In New England people lived for an average of around 40 years. (This was comparable to the average life span in Britain at the same time.) In the Chesapeake colonies (including Maryland and Virginia), where malaria and tropical diseases were a factor, the average person lived for only 25 to 30 years. For poor people with inadequate diets, little protection from harsh winters, constant hard work, and little access to medical care, average life span was much lower. The mortality rates for infants and women during childbirth were extremely high. As was discussed earlier, many new immigrants weakened by their long sea voyage died within weeks of reaching America. Many indentured servants failed to survive their period of servitude. Slave life expectancy in the colonies was shorter than whites but higher than for slaves on Caribbean sugar plantations. Epidemics such as smallpox regularly decimated the population of towns and cities.

A Christian burial

One of the preoccupations of the poor was obtaining a respectable Christian burial. The alterative was an unmarked pauper's grave in the "potter's field," or public burial ground. An unusual insight into early American burial practices has

ABOVE: **Wood engraving of a country gravestone, 1800.**

LEFT: **"Poor Man's Burial" by Pierre Roch Vogneron shows a pauper's burial. The poor were often buried in unmarked graves or mass graves, even though the greatest hope of many was a decent Christian burial after they died.**

been provided by the church records of Gloria Dei Swedish Lutheran church in Philadelphia, where the pastor, Nicholas Collin, kept detailed accounts from 1791 to 1809. Scholars such as Susan Klepp and Simon Newman have recently researched these records. Klepp estimates that more than a quarter of the people who applied to bury a relative at church lacked sufficient money to pay for interment in hallowed ground. In many cases the minister agreed to reduce or waive burial fees, or assistance for burial was sought from poor-relief officials. Newman cites a few of these cases, noting that relatives or even the dying person would plead with the pastor. Collin recorded, for example, that 29-year-old Mary Ryan:

> "Requested on her death bed to be buried in our cemetery, where 2 of her children had been interred."

The importance of a Christian burial was revealed by the many instances in which poor African Americans—who were earlier "warned out" by poor relief officers—were granted aid in their final days to obtain a suitable grave. Many religious and secular charitable societies of the time had as their principal aim the financing of a respectable burial for the poor.

The same church records provide further details of the life and death of the poor in Philadelphia. More than two-thirds of the adult males who died and were buried at Gloria Dei were sailors, or they worked in related occupations such as ships' carpenters or riggers. Most of the remaining men buried there had been low-level artisans or apprentices. Almost half of all those buried in the cemetery were children under five years old. Just one in 20 was an adult over 60. Reflecting the extremely high rates of infant mortality, the average age of those who died in this crowded and poverty-stricken district was only 18.

NATIVE AMERICAN BURIAL PRACTICES

Native American burial practices differed substantially from those of the Christian European colonists, for whom a Christian burial was vitally important. These images show two different Native American burials. The first (TOP) is a Timucuan ceremony in Florida in 1591, with the tribe surrounding a conch shell encircled by arrows. The second (ABOVE) shows a Native American woman bringing sustenance to a dead relative lying on a burial platform.

Private charitable societies played an important role in caring for the poor and underprivileged of early America. This was especially true starting in the mid-1700s, when the limitations of the overtaxed public poor-relief system became apparent.

The first private relief group in the colonies was the Scots' Charitable Society. Twenty-seven persons of Scottish origin established the group in Boston in 1657 for the "releefe of our selves or any other for which wee may see cause." With only a lapse from 1667 to 1684 the Scots' society has continued in existence to this day. Financed by wealthy merchants, the group paid for the care of countrymen who were sick, maintained those who would have otherwise needed poor relief, and gave a respectable burial to the dead. It became the model for numerous other societies organized on national, religious, or occupational lines in the eighteenth century. In Boston Anglicans founded the Episcopal Charitable Society in 1724, while the Charitable Irish Society of Boston was set up in 1737. Charleston had a St. Andrew's Society for the Scots starting in 1730, an English St. George's Society in 1736, and a French Huguenots South Carolina Society in 1737. Participation in one or more of these societies, which often held elegant

RIGHT: **A family of beggars. Charitable societies played an important role alongside poor relief officials in aiding the impoverished. In particular, many provided access to basic schooling for poor children.**

dinners for their patrons, became a feature of high society. At the same time, their aid became a vital supplement to public relief.

Marine aid societies

Given the importance of maritime trade to all the colonies, it is not surprising that the earliest of the many occupationally based charitable societies were established to support infirm or retired sailors and their families. Sailors were poorly paid, badly fed, and worked in extremely dangerous conditions. Crippling injuries, disease, and death were a constant threat to them and their families. Sailors were often not paid when their ships were in port because it was cheaper to hire day laborers for dock work. Even when mariners were employed, their families were often forced to rely on poor relief when they were at sea for long voyages. Injury and the cumulative effect of many hard years left many sailors unable to work. A typical example was the sailor Thomas Loudon, admitted to the Philadelphia almshouse on 1800. The clerk noted that:

"Casualties and accidents in his way of life, and the vicissitudes of fortune to which such men are liable seems now to manifest itself."

The first maritime charitable organization was the Boston Marine Society, founded as The Fellowship Club in June 1742. Membership was restricted to present and former ship's captains, and its object was to meet the needs of its own members who fell on hard times and to assist other needy mariners. It was followed by marine societies in Salem in 1766, New York in 1769, Newburyport in 1772, Portland in 1796, and Portsmouth in 1808.

In addition there were other philanthropic associations established by well-meaning individuals to assist particular groups of poor people—for example, providing a school for poor children or employment to distressed widows. The Female Benevolent Society in Raleigh, North Carolina, founded a school in 1823 and noted in its bylaws:

"The Education of Poor Children is a very important object with this Society. This branch of it has already produced good fruits, where all before was barren and unprofitable. To the children themselves, the advantages are incalculable, and the community will be fully remunerated for its charitable contributions by the improved morals, industrious habits, and regular conduct of these youthful objects of benevolence."

Like others in early America, many charitable societies changed their ideas about the poor during the eighteenth century. Their objectives often began to focus on reforming the impoverished—much like officials at workhouses. The Philadelphia "House of Industry" established in 1798 by the Quaker ladies of the Female Society for the Relief and Employment of the Poor (founded 1795) reflected these theories but seems to have been sensitive to the reality of poor women's lives:

"Having had frequent opportunities of observing the difficulties many of the poor labor under who take work to their own homes, owing to the smallness of their rooms, want of fuels, and embarrassment [inconvenience] of their children, We are induced to believe a benefit would arise in providing a house containing several commodious apartments, purchasing a quantity of flax, wool, some large and small Wheels and other utensils necessary to spinning and appropriating one of the rooms and such utensils to

PHILANTHROPISTS

Portrait of philanthropist Paul P. Beck (1760–1844). Charitable giving was considered a moral obligation by many wealthy Americans who funded many eighteenth-century institutions.

the use of a number of spinners who might be made comfortable by one fire and supplied with food at a much lower rate than would be possible by distributing a portion to each family."

What the women who benefited from such well-intentioned assistance thought of this arrangement was unfortunately not recorded. In fact, the idea would have been doomed to failure because it ignored the wider economics of textile production at the time. Small-scale production in rural homes was being replaced by factories, meaning spinning yarn was not a viable occupation for an individual. This failure to see the bigger picture was typical of charitable relief efforts both private and public. Sadly they often incorrectly placed the blame for unemployment and poverty on individuals.

War was the ultimate challenge to those on the brink of poverty; it even threatened those from the settled middle class. The loss of the main income earner to the military could throw a family on relief even if the men were not killed or disabled.

LEFT: **By the end of the American Revolution 11,000 Patriot prisoners had died aboard British prison ships anchored in American harbors.**

Farms and settlements were frequently plundered and burned. Attack from Native Americans was a continual threat in frontier districts, as this 1757 petition from Hanover, Pennsylvania, shows:

> "Sir: We, in these parts, are at present in the utmost Confusion, the Savage Enemy has again fallen on us afresh. Yesterday morning early they plundered the house of Alexander Martin, & carried his mother Captive, & this morning early they killed Thomas Bell, an honest responsible Dweller on the Frontier, within forty yards of his own house.
>
> "…In these our distressed Circumstances, the greater part of the remaining Inhabitants are now flying with wives & Children to places more remote from Danger…we who continue must either fall a sacrifice to our Enemies Cruelty, or go with our wives and Children to beg our Bread.
>
> "We beg the favour of you to represent our distressed case to his Honour the Governour, if we may obtain some assistance of men for our defence, as the Provincials, now stationed here, are of no benefit here."

Many refugees flooded towns and overwhelmed poor-relief systems. Food shortages resulted from blockades or the need to provision British troops and sometimes led to food rioting, such as in Boston in 1709 and 1713. Disrupted trade patterns led to unemployment for sailors and numerous other craftsmen who sustained the ports.

In the aftermath of wars returning soldiers struggled to rebuild families during trade downturns. They often joined the swollen ranks of the able-bodied poor—the so-called "sturdy beggars"—wandering from town to town seeking work and excluded from poor relief. Patriot General Nathanael Greene wrote in 1781:

> "The loss of our army in Charleston, and the defeat of General Gates has been the cause of keeping such vast shoals of militia on foot, who like the locusts of Egypt, have eaten up everything, and the expense has been so enormous, that it has ruined the currency of the State….We are living upon charity, and subsist by daily collections. Indian meal and beef is our common diet, and not a drop of spirits have we had with us since I came to the army."

During the French and Indian War the British relocated 5,000 Acadians (French colonists in the New World) from Canada. They endured harsh conditions as refugees in the colonies. In Philadelphia many lived on the city's edge in crude huts built by Quaker volunteers. The Acadians were prevented from entering the city for fear that they would spread disease. Almost half of the Acadians died from starvation and cold before adequate aid was approved.

Soldiers fighting in the war also suffered terrible conditions. Private Obadiah Harris served with Massachusetts troops north of Albany in 1758 and complained in his diary:

"We Eate up all Clean that was in our Tents and whare to get the Next Mouthfull we Know not but hope that Providence will provide for us. Now men are so Cross and tachey [touchy] that they can't Speak to one and other What shall we do for Sumthing to Eate is the Crye."

The Revolutionary War mobilized two opposing armies whose size had never been seen before in the Americas. The war caused great destruction and numerous casualties, but simply supporting such large forces also led to widespread suffering. Inflation, hoarding, and profiteering created food shortages and hunger in the cities. The troops on both sides were inadequately clothed and fed, especially during the harsh winters, and many died as a result of hunger and disease. Camped at Valley Forge during the winter of 1777, George Washington's army of 12,000 lost 2,000 to 3,000 men. A mixture of flour and water known as "firecake" was the main ration. Surgeon Albigence Waldo noted in his diary:

"There comes a Soldier, his bare feet are seen thro' his worn out Shoes, his legs nearly naked from the tatter'd remains of an only pair of stockings, his Breeches not sufficient to cover his nakedness,

WASHINGTON BURNS

War brought terrible suffering to both soldiers and civilians—and not only through direct action but also through disease, famine, and destruction of property. These two views show the British attack on Washington, D.C., during the War of 1812, in which the attackers set fire to both the Capitol and the White House.

his Shirt hanging in Strings, his hair dishevell'd, his face meagre; his whole appearance pictures a person forsaken and discouraged. He comes, and crys with an air of wretchedness and despair, I am Sick, my feet lame, my legs are sore, my body cover'd with this tormenting Itch—my Cloaths are worn out, my Constitution is broken, my former Activity is exhausted by fatigue, hunger and Cold, I fail fast I shall soon be no more!"

Typhus, typhoid, dysentery, and pneumonia swept through the cold and malnourished men. The injured and prisoners fared even worse. It is said that the men held by the British in Walnut Street Jail in Philadelphia ate rats and grass roots to survive. Up to a dozen starved to death each day and were buried in mass graves in what is now Washington Square.

It might surprise us today to learn that there was poverty in rural areas of colonial America as well as in the slums of the growing cities. Access to land was seen as the key to achieving wealth and status in early America.

LEFT: **Settlement on the Virginian frontier. The settlers' thrust westward was necessitated by the lack of free farming land in the east.**

RIGHT: **Country entertainment—men and women dance and drink in a country tavern, while a seated man plays the violin, 1814. To many, taverns were also seen as centers of gambling and other vices that distracted poor people from honest labor.**

A hardworking family could move from poverty to wealth on land that they had cleared, plowed, and planted. This was perhaps the ultimate expression of the American dream. Adapting the farming skills of Europe to the new climate and conditions was not easy, particularly for inexperienced farmers. They learned their trade the hard way, through trial and error. Ultimately many never became wealthy, and life continued to be hard. Writing in 1813 about the "Yankee farmer," a commentator noted:

"He can mend his plough, erect his wall…thrash his corn, handle his axe, his hoe, his scythe, his saw, break a colt or drive a team with equal address; being habituated from early life to rely on himself he acquires a skill in every branch of his profession which is unknown in countries where labor is more divided."

For many farming alone did not provide sufficient income to maintain a family. Family members who could be spared from farm work often took on crafts such as weaving cloth to make extra money. Thomas Cooper, traveling through the U.S. in the 1790s, noted:

"The union of manufactures and farming [was] very convenient on the grain farmers where part of every day and a great part of the year can be spared from the business of the farm and employed in some mechanical, handycraft or manufacturing business."

Some insight into this pioneer farming lifestyle is given by the memories of Pharaoh Jackson Chesney (born 1781), an early resident of the territory that became the state of Tennessee:

"While the children would gather around the wide fire-place and pick cotton from the seeds; the mother or eldest daughter would be spinning thread; some one would be carding rolls; the father, apt as not, would be making a pair of shoes; a split basket, or 'bottoming' a chair with splits. Sometimes the mother's 'evening job' would be knitting, and when she would pay her neighbor a visit, she would invariably take her knitting along….But each member of the family, unless it was the baby, had

some kind of work, and no one left the circle until one of the parents called out 'bed-time.' There were no lamps, and as a rule, the room was lighted by huge pine knots brought from a neighboring ridge. Often, however, home-made candles were used. These were made by pouring melted beef tallow into moulds in which a wick had been suspended."

Speculators and the landless

Great wealth during this period came not from the proceeds of farming but from owning—or speculating in—large quantities of land. Access to land was the driving force of westward expansion as people without land searched for new prospects on the frontier. Consider this letter from the frontier (in what is now Mississippi) describing the availability of land:

"I have met with I suppose from 50 to 100 men who (many of them are entirely destitute of a common education) five years since could not get credit for a pair of shoes, now worth 100,000 to a million of dollars....It is in truth the only country I ever read or heard of, where a poor man could in 2 or 3 years without any aid, become wealthy. A few days of labor and lying out in the woods enabled them to find out a good body of land, and not having the money to enter it for themselves, they would sell their information to those who were too idle, or too rich to undergo the fatigue of hunting for it; by this means they would obtain money enough to enter one section, then two, and so on; soon sell that for ten or twenty times as much as they gave for it."

This letter describes not farming but land speculation. Land speculation occurs when a person or a company obtains title to a large amount of land, sometimes through questionable means. Then they hold onto this land, hoping to sell it for a profit in the future. Land speculation was a problem in both the original colonies and in new areas as they were opened up to settlement. Usually a small minority of people quickly established control over, and ownership of, most of the land.

There were usually huge obstacles in the way of the poor people obtaining any

LEFT: **It's October and harvest season in 1810. Farmers have gathered the apple crop and are shown squeezing the liquid out of the fruit with a cider press.**

BELOW: **A farmer leads his horse-drawn harrow. The life of the subsistence farmer was a tough one, filled with year-round backbreaking labor trying to produce enough food to feed his family.**

land of their own. While some poor white immigrants, such as the Palatine redemptioners who settled in Pennsylvania, acquired land they could farm, too many others were left out. Those not able to buy their own land included most former indentured servants as well as free African Americans. For those who wanted to be farmers, the alternative was tenant farming, also known as sharecropping. In this system tenants were allowed to live on and farm land but had to pay the landowner rent in the form of most of their harvest.

Throughout the colonies leading families who already owned large tracts of land also—by virtue of their wealth and social position—controlled the colonial assemblies and town authorities. They were generally ruthless and sometimes corrupt in exploiting their authority to add to their land holdings. By the 1770s virtually all land in the established colonies was privately owned, with a small number of families owning vast estates. Most people without land also lacked sufficient money to buy and develop land even when it became available. Lack of money also stopped many people from moving to the open frontier because they could not buy the tools and other provisions needed to clear and farm the land.

In the South most of the land was divided into vast plantations worked by slaves growing tobacco, rice, or indigo. At this time there was no tradition of wage labor, even for landowners who did not rely solely on slaves. Sometimes they used indentured servants and a smaller number of slaves to work as field hands. More frequently they leased out plots to tenant farmers.

Poverty and tenant farmers

In some areas, with good fortune and good weather, it was possible to make a modestly successful living as a tenant farmer. Sometimes they were even able to save enough money to purchase their own land. Small-scale farmers in the

REAPING HOOK

ABOVE: **A typical early American farmyard shows a farmer by his barn feeding livestock.**

seventeenth and eighteenth centuries used crude wooden hand tools with metal blades, along with animal-drawn plows. Children and sometimes a single indentured servant or slave provided the labor. Most of the crop was used to feed the family. In good years a small surplus might be available to sell. Alongside cattle and sheep farmers in New England grew corn, rye, and oats, as well as fruit and vegetables. In New Jersey, New York, and Pennsylvania wheat was the main crop.

This biggest problem with tenant farming, even in fertile areas, was insecurity. Every year the tenant had to pay the agreed quantity of crops, or else the value of those crops, to the landowner. If they failed to pay, they could be evicted. Illness, injury, or bad weather were constant threats to their success. Tenants were reluctant to improve the land because they could be evicted and the landlords benefit from their hard work. Good landlords allowed

tenants some flexibility to make up debts from difficult years, but evictions were still frequent, as was conflict. Attempts to evict tenants were often met by bands of farmers who refused landlords and officials access to the land.

Tenant farmers rioted alongside the landless in New York, New Jersey, and New England starting as early as the 1750s. Some radical tenants claimed that their years of labor entitled them to own their lands. Unrest reached a peak during a rebellion by several hundred tenants of the Van Rensselaer estates in New York in 1765. The conflict had to be put down by British troops. After the Revolutionary War, in 1786, around 2,000 indebted farmers from western Massachusetts formed the core of a rebellion against the government. A former Revolutionary Army captain named Daniel Shays led this armed protest against laws that were thought to be unfair to farmers and workers. There was considerable sympathy for the

grievances of the rebels, as this letter from Thomas Jefferson makes clear:

"I hold it that a little rebellion now and then is a good thing, and as necessary in the political world as storms in the physical. Unsuccessful rebellions, indeed, generally establish the encroachments on the rights of the people which have produced them. An observation of this truth should render honest republican governors so mild in their punishment of rebellions as not to discourage them too much. It is a medicine necessary for the sound health of the government."

Reverend John Barnard's childhood memories reveal that school life in early America was very different from today.

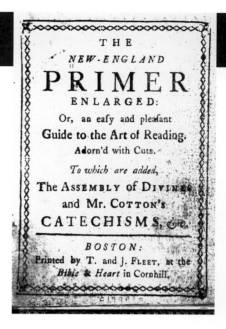

"I was born at Boston, 6th Nov. 1681; descended from reputable parents, viz. John and Esther Barnard, remarkable for their piety and benevolence, who devoted me to the service of God, in the work of the ministry, from my very conception and birth; and accordingly took special care to instruct me themselves in the principles of the Christian religion, and kept me close at school to furnish my young mind with the knowledge of letters. By that time I had a little passed my sixth year, I had left my reading-school, in the latter part of which my mistress made me a sort of usher, appointing me to teach some children that were older than myself, as well as smaller ones; and in which time I had read my Bible through thrice. My parents thought me to be weakly, because of my thin habit and pale countenance, and therefore sent me into the country, where I spent my seventh summer, and by the change of air and diet and exercise I grew more fleshy and hardy; and that I might not lose my reading, was put to a school-mistress, and returned home in the fall."

Schools were extremely small, generally a single room or a front parlor with just one teacher. Many, known as "dame schools," were run by women who took children aged between about 5 and 10 years old at their home for a few hours a day and tried to teach them to read. Local leaders in the colonies often placed a high value on literacy and learning. For example a high proportion of children in Massachusetts received at least a basic education because Puritan leaders wanted citizens to be able to read the Bible and other religious texts. Early in the colony's history leaders passed an ambitious law that spelled out the requirements of education. The law also called for a stiff fine for failing to educate their children and servants. It also gave the selectmen (elected town leaders) the power to take away children or servants who were not receiving an appropriate education:

"Forasmuch as the good education of children is of singular behoof [advantage] and benefit to any Common-wealth; and whereas many parents & masters are too indulgent and negligent of their duty in that kind. It is therefore ordered that the Select men of every town, in the several precincts and quarters

ABOVE: **The cover of *The New England Primer*, an elementary textbook used in America around the time of the Revolutionary War.**

RIGHT: **Rock School in New Canaan, Connecticut, built in 1799.**

BELOW RIGHT: **A primer designed to be used Mohawk children. It was published in London in 1786. The easternmost tribe of the Iroquois League, the Mohawks were friends of the British during the eighteenth century and following the Revolutionary War moved to Canada.**

where they dwell, shall have a vigilant eye over their brethren & neighbours, to see, first that none of them shall suffer so much barbarism in any of their families as not to endeavour to teach by themselves or others, their children & apprentices so much learning as may enable them perfectly to read the English tongue, & knowledge of the Capital Laws: upon penalty of twenty shillings for each neglect therein. Also that all masters of families do once a week (at the least) catechize their children and

servants in the grounds & principles of Religion, & if any be unable to doe so much: that then at the least they procure such children or apprentices to learn some short orthodox catechism without book, that they may be able to answer unto the questions that shall be propounded to them out of such catechism by their parents or masters or any of the Select men when they shall call them to a trial of what they have learned of this kind. And further that all parents and masters do breed & bring up their children & apprentices in some honest lawful calling, labour or employment, either in husbandry, or some other trade profitable for themselves, and the Common-wealth if they will not or cannot train them up in learning to fit them for higher employments. And if any of the Select men after

admonition by them given to such masters of families shall find them still negligent of their duty in the particulars aforementioned, whereby children and servants become rude, stubborn & unruly;

the said Select men with the help of two Magistrates, or the next County court for that Shire, shall take such children or apprentices from them & place them with some masters for years (boys till they come to twenty

A

PRIMER,

FOR THE USE OF THE

MOHAWK CHILDREN,

To acquire the SPELLING and READING of their OWN, as well as to get acquainted with the ENGLISH, Tongue; which for that Purpose is put on the opposite Page.

WAERIGHWAGHSAWE IKSAONGOENWA

Tſiwaondad-derighhonny Kaghyadoghſera; Nayon-deweyeſtaghk ayeweanaghnòdon ayeghyàdow Ka-niyenkehàga Kaweanondaghkouh; Dyorheaf-hàga oni tſinihadiweanotea.

LONDON,
PRINTED BY C. BUCKTON, GREAT PULTNEY-STREET.
1786.

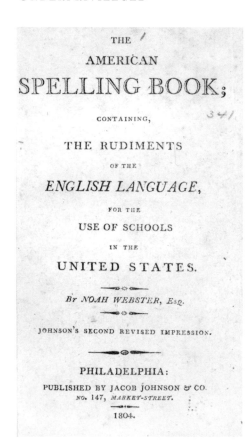

THE

AMERICAN

SPELLING BOOK;

CONTAINING,

THE RUDIMENTS

OF THE

ENGLISH LANGUAGE,

FOR THE

USE OF SCHOOLS

IN THE

UNITED STATES.

By NOAH WEBSTER, Esq.

JOHNSON'S SECOND REVISED IMPRESSION.

PHILADELPHIA:

PUBLISHED BY JACOB JOHNSON & CO.
NO. 147, MARKET-STREET.

1804.

one, and girls eighteen years of age complete) which will more strictly look unto, and force them to submit unto government according to the rules of this order, if by fair means and former instructions they will not be drawn into it."

Although the goals of the law were not always reached, the law helped enforce the colony's commitment to education. As the excerpt from the widely used school primer below indicates, this education was focused on teaching the moral values thought to be essential in life.

During the early colonial era there were a number of tax-supported public primary schools in Massachusetts and Rhode Island. There were also schools run by religious denominations. At least some poor children were able to attend

these schools thanks to the help of public or private charity, although until 1789 free schooling in Boston was only open to boys. Although reading was regarded as important for both boys and girls, the same did not apply to writing. Reading was essential for a full Christian life because it gave direct access to the Bible, but writing seems to have been regarded more as a vocational skill that would allow boys to work as clerks or bookkeepers but was not likely to be useful for poor women. Instead, the emphasis for them was on sewing.

Primary education for African American children was rare and usually relied on the efforts of private citizens or groups. For example, the Quakers in Philadelphia ran two schools that were open to both free African Americans and slaves. The poor were largely excluded from secondary education, which was

THE NEW ENGLAND PRIMER: AN ALPHABET OF LESSONS FOR YOUTH

The *New-England* PRIMER IMPROVED;

For the more eafy attaining the true Reading of ENGLISH.

To WHICH IS ADDED;

The ASSEMBLY of DIVINES, and Mr. COTTON'S CATECHISM

PROVIDENCE
Printed and Sold by JOHN CAR-ER, at *Shakefpear's Head.* 1775.

A Wise son maketh a glad father, but a foolish son is the heaviness of his mother.

Better is a little with the fear of the Lord, than great treasure & trouble therewith.

Come unto Christ all ye that labor and are heavy laden and he will give you rest.

Do not the abominable thing which I hate saith the Lord.

Except a man be born again, he cannot see the kingdom of God.

Foolishness is bound up in the heart of a child, but the rod of correction shall drive it far from him.

Godliness is profitable unto all things, having the promise of the life that now is, and that which is to come.

Holiness becomes god's house for ever.

It is good for me to draw near unto god.

[J omitted in original]

Keep thy heart with all diligence, for out of it are the issues of life.

Liars shall have their part in the lake which burns with fire and brimstone.

Many are the afflictions of the righteous, but the lord delivereth them out of them all.

Now is the accepted time, now is the day of salvation.

Out of the abundance of the heart the mouth speaketh.

Pray to thy Father which is in secret; and thy Father which sees in secret shall reward thee openly.

Quit you like men, be strong, stand fast in the faith.

Remember thy Creator in the days of thy youth.

Seest thou a man wise in his own conceit, there is more hope of a fool than of him.

Trust in God at all times, ye people, pour out your hearts before him.

Upon the wicked, God shall rain an horrible tempest.

[V omitted in original]

Wo to the wicked, it shall be ill with him, for the reward of his hands shall be given him.

eXhort one another daily while it is called to day, lest any of you be hardened thro' the deceitfulness of sin.

Young men ye have overcome the wicked one.

Zeal hath consumed me, because thy enemies have forgotten the word of God.

ABOVE LEFT: **This book taught the basics of spelling and the English language. Written by Noah Webster, it was published in Philadelphia in 1804.**

LEFT: **A school for African American children in Richmond, Virginia. Primary education for African Americans was rare and tended to be financed by philanthropists or religious groups.**

much less developed. Secondary schools, particularly the more ambitious ones that taught Latin and prepared youths for higher education, were usually reserved for middle- and upper-class boys. Girls from wealthier families were sometimes given private tutoring. In Pennsylvania, New York, New Jersey, and the southern colonies churches took the lead in running schools. The standards for educating the poor and the opportunities made available to them varied from colony to colony. Pennsylvania was considered the most progressive colony in educating the poor, while schools in South Carolina were generally regarded as inadequate.

66 This manufactory will go into operation in all this month, where a number of boys and girls, from eight to twelve years of age, are wanted, to whom constant employment and encouraging wages will be given. **99**

This advertisement by the Baltimore Cotton Manufactory seeking child workers appeared in the *Federal Gazette* (Baltimore), January 4, 1808.

Other volumes in this set look at the day-to-day details of working life in early America, at what is was like to be a tailor, a dock worker, a chimney sweep, or a laundrymaid. Our concern here is to consider how employment was related to poverty. Did working men and women have comfortable lives? Or were they, like the unemployed, constantly struggling to overcome poverty and insecurity? Why did the children of working people also have to work to sustain the family?

We have seen that in early America able-bodied men and women who were unable to find employment often found themselves dependent on poor relief. As the eighteenth century went on, they were more likely to be confined to a public workhouse. Their children were often taken away and bound out as servants to other families. They were regarded by leaders of public opinion as lazy and morally irresponsible. If they

ABOVE: **A farmer sowing. Working life on the land was almost always long, backbreaking, and did not always provide sufficient resources to feed a large family.**

LEFT: **Illustration for a story entitled "Maria—A Sentimental Fragment," set on a Massachusetts farm in 1796. It shows the traditional requirements for milkmaids.**

RIGHT: **The Blue Anchor Inn, Philadelphia, in 1776. With the fire burning and a full table, this gives an impression of wealth and good times—but running a tavern wasn't always a certain way to prosperity (see panel on page 66).**

traveled in search of work, they could be whipped and "warned out" of a community. In contrast, those who found work were regarded as models of moral living and virtuous self-improvement. In the words of Benjamin Franklin:

"If we are industrious we shall never starve; for, as Poor Richard says, At the working Man's House Hunger looks in, but dares not enter....God gives all Things to Industry."

Work and insecurity

In fact, those employed in the lower-paid occupations in early America were often the same people who were at other times on poor relief. For all except the disabled, sick, and elderly poor, relief was supposed to be a short-term measure. The recipient was expected to find paying work as soon as possible. Their options included working on the docks, on farms, and in industries such as shipbuilding, lumbering, milling, and tanning. In most of these trades demand for labor was seasonal. Work was available for only part of the year even when the economy was booming. Winter, when life was often the toughest, was a difficult time to find work. As a result many working people were not far removed from people on poor relief. Many moved on and off charity rolls depending on the season and on life's circumstances.

Free blacks often found life even more challenging. They had to overcome discrimination while competing against both white workers and slave craftsmen. Opportunities to make a decent living were usually rare.

At the same time, there were men and a few women who had marketable skills, usually as a result of an indentured apprenticeship in a craft trade such as printing, blacksmithing, hatmaking, or—for women—dressmaking. Many were able to establish an independent business with a reliable customer base, but this required modest capital and both skill and good fortune. Many succeeded but were still vulnerable to illness, injury, fire, economic downturn, and the other incidents of life. Insecurity remained a constant feature of working life at this time.

As the eighteenth century went on, the labor market changed. More working people were left insecure and poor despite the colonies' economic growth. In particular there was a decline in the use of indentured labor, which was replaced by journeymen paid on day or "piece" rates (that is, so much for each item finished). After the Revolution this change accelerated. In part this was due to an economic downturn during which wage rates for day laborers fell and the cost of indentures rose. In the bigger picture it was part of a growing trend away from small-scale production toward industrialization.

Child labor

Industrialization, which was more widely felt in the nineteenth century, paved the way for adding more children to the workforce. Poor children had always worked in early America as they

A WORKER'S EXPERIENCES

As with the recipients of poor relief there are few direct accounts of worker's experiences from this period. One rare survival is an autobiography published by Thurlow Weed, who became a printer in Boston in the nineteenth century. Of particular interest to us is the account he left of his haphazard series of jobs from the age of eight:

"My first employment, when about eight years old, was in blowing a blacksmith's bellows for a Mr. Reeves, who gave me six cents per day, which contributed so much towards the support of the family....My next service was in the capacity of boy of all work, at a tavern in the village of Jefferson…kept by a Captain Baker, who had, I remember, made a great mistake in exchanging the command of a ship for a tavern. After the sheriff took possession of Captain Baker's wrecked hotel, I got a situation as cabin boy on board the sloop *Ranger*, Captain Grant. This gratified a desire I had to see the city of New York. I was then (1806) in my ninth year.…In the fall and winter of 1808, I was equivocally [uncertainly] attached to the office of the 'Catskill Recorder.' I say equivocally, because I was not regularly apprenticed, and yet I carried the paper to the village subscribers, and did 'chores' about the office, with a strong desire and hope that I should be received as an apprentice. Late that autumn [1809] I was rejoiced with the information that printing materials had arrived at Onondaga Hollow, where a newspaper was to be published. My father, anxious to see me in the way of learning a trade, gratified my own wishes by making an application in my behalf as an apprentice.…My first employment as an apprentice, beside cutting wood and making fires in the printing-office, was in 'treading pelts,' a duty of which the present generation of printers is growing up in ignorance."

is supplied to so many poor children. But an eloquence was exerted on the other side of the question more commanding than this, which calls us to pity those little creatures, plying in a contracted room, among flyers and coggs, at an age when nature requires for them air, space and sports. There was a dull dejection in the countenance of all of them."

did in other countries, but with growing factory production child labor became more formal and routine. At the time most people regarded child labor as a good thing that freed communities from some of their financial support for poor families. Josiah Quincy, mayor of Boston and president of Harvard University, expressed concern for child workers:

"All the processes of turning cotton from its rough into every variety of marketable thread state, such as cleaning, carding, spinning, winding, etc., are here performed by machinery operating by water wheels only by children from four to ten years old, and one superintendent. Above one hundred of the former are employed at the rate of from 12 to 25 cents for a day's labor. Our attendant was very eloquent on the usefulness of this manufacture, and the employment

Another effect of the shift away from indentured labor was a growing number of disputes over wages and piecework prices. Day laborers and craftsmen tried to defend their precarious position by forming associations and guilds to bargain collectively with employers or attempt to fix prices. These groups developed into trade unions later in the nineteenth century, but at this time their activities were often regarded as illegal.

One such incident occurred in

Philadelphia in 1806 when a group of shoemakers (then known as cord-wainers) were tried on charges of forming an illegal association to fix prices. The court testimony preserves a rare account by a workingman, Job Harrison, of his struggle to survive. He could not afford to join the strike that was threatened. If he stopped work, his family would have been forced into the Bettering House:

"At that time I was from hand to mouth, and in debt, owing to the sickness of my family, and market work was only [paying] from 3 schilling to 3 schilling 6 pence per pair. I concluded at that time I would turn a scab [strike breaker], unknown to them, and I would continue my work and not let them know of it.…I had a neighbor, who I was acquainted with, and thought a good deal of, I knew I could not deceive him.…He was a shoemaker and upon the turn-out. I said to him Swain, you know my circumstances, my family must perish, or go to the bettering house, unless I continue my work."

ABOVE: **Farm laborers cut flax in this woodcut from around 1810.**

LEFT: **A 1787 comic cut shows a group of chimney sweeps laughing as a servant girl drops a plate on Lombard Street in Philadelphia.**

As Boston, New York, and the other eighteenth-century American cities grew, they experienced an increase in crime.

ABOVE: **An anti-British protest against the Stamp Act—"England's Folly." Middle- and upper-class disaffection with taxes led to the Revolution.**

Alarmist newspaper opinions often blamed either the poor or the many British convicts serving indentures in the colonies for growing crime. In reality poor people were far from being responsible for all the criminal activity. They were the victims of crime, and they also committed many crimes. An excerpt from Massachusetts colony court records describes the type of crime encountered in seventeenth-century America:

"Henry Spencer confessed in court that he ran away from his master, Edmond Mounforth, and stole from him a coat, a piece of serge [fabric], 2 Bibles, a rapier [sword] and belt, a pewter bottle and a piece of linen cloth, and being at Andover at Goodman Chandlour's, he broke into said Chandlour's house twice and stole a horse and saddle. After being apprehended and brought to Ipswich prison, he broke prison. He was ordered to be severely whipped, branded on the forehead with the letter B, and pay a fine of five pounds to the county, and to his master, treble damages, amounting to thirteen pounds, and forty shillings to his master for loss of time. Further ordered that upon his master paying the fine, he should be sent to Boston prison, there to remain until his master can dispose of him. In the meantime, he was to be kept in Ipswich prison.

"John Palmer, for his high misdemeanor in attempting uncleanness with Elizabeth White in her master's house, was ordered to be severely whipped and to pay costs to Mr. Epps.

"John Kent was ordered to be whipped or to pay a fine for fornication [adultery].

"John Cheny, presented for reviling [abusive] speeches, was fined.

"Robert Morse and Susana Rogers, presented for reviling words, were fined.

"John Leigh, jr., was fined for threatening words against Sam Younglove.

"Mary Williams forfeited her bond for appearance, and she was ordered to be whipped unless she pay the bond or 3li. in money.

"Margret Allexander, for fornication, was to be whipped. Upon payment of a fine the corporal punishment was remitted.

"Thomas Bettes, servant to John Simmons, often running away and being incorrigible [unmanageable], said Simmons was discharged of his obligation of teaching the trade of a weaver.

"Mr. William Godswell having taken Thomas Bettes, who was sentenced to be whipped, and paying 40s. [schillings] said Bettes had his corporal punishment remitted, and in consideration of his master Cogswell buying off his whipping, he agreed to serve him one year more than the time of his indenture and the six months ordered to serve his master Simmons by Ipswich court, Mar. 29, 1682. Jo. Sparke was allowed charges.

"Phillip Fowler was presented for abusing his servant, Richard Parker, and although court justified any person in giving meet [proper] correction to his servant, which the boy deserved, yet they did not approve of the manner of punishment given in hanging him up by the heels as butchers do beasts for the slaughter, and cautioned said Fowler against such kind of punishment. He was ordered to pay costs."

The records reveal that early American courts were just as interested in managing relations between masters and servants and policing sexual behavior as they were in punishing crimes such as theft, counterfeiting, and murder. Servants who ran away, stole from, or otherwise breached contracts with their masters were often whipped and had more time added to their service period. There were, however, limits to the acceptable treatment of servants. Phillip Fowler appears to have exceeded these limits by suspending a boy upside down by his heels to punish him.

At the start of the eighteenth century Boston, Charleston, New York, and Philadelphia were little more than small towns. Almost everyone knew each other, and common crimes were domestic disputes, failure to observe the Sabbath, and immorality. A century later they were cities almost equal to the largest in Europe. They had poor and overcrowded slums and typical urban problems, including street crime, burglary, and prostitution. The port districts, with their disreputable taverns filled with sailors and new, poor immigrants, concerned city officials.

Cities did not have the resources to deal with these problems. Undermanned, untrained night watchmen were the only type of police force. Jails were small and poorly maintained. Criminals shared space with imprisoned debtors, and the few serious criminals captured often escaped. In New York the jail was at City Hall on Broad Street, along with a whipping post and pillory in which criminals were exposed to public anger. One inmate in 1766 complained that there was:

"Nothing but the bare floor to lay on—no covering—almost devoured with all kinds of Vermin."

Riot and rebellion

As noted earlier, tenant farmers sometimes resorted to organized revolts to resist evictions and unfair rent—Shays' Rebellion was one such example. In the cities dissatisfaction among the middle and upper classes with British taxation eventually led to the Revolution. Among the poor there were many smaller incidents of unrest by people who felt excluded from the prosperity of the colonies. Food riots broke out in Boston and other ports in 1710 and 1713 when merchants tried to profit from shortages by hoarding and exporting grain. There were land riots in New York and New Jersey in the 1730s and in the Carolinas in the 1760s, riots over changes to public market regulations in Boston in the 1730s, and riots over elections in Philadelphia in 1742.

City officials were concerned that both the working poor and the unemployed could, if provoked, form dangerous and unpredictable "mobs." However, it usually took a specific event to focus anger, rather than just general discontent. By the 1760s a few radical leaders emerged who made wider attacks on the inequalities of American life. Among them was James Otis, who, along with John Adams, was a prominent agitator against British taxation prior to the Revolution. He charged that the wealthy of Boston:

ABOVE: **A convict and his coffin approach the scaffold where he will be hanged—the ultimate price for unrest and revolt.**

"Grind the faces of the poor without remorse, eat the bread of oppression without fear, and wax fat on the spoils of the people."

There were also numerous attempted slave revolts: in Gloucester County, Virginia, in 1663; in New York in 1712 and 1741; in Stono, South Carolina, in 1739; Prosser's rebellion in Richmond, Virginia, in 1800; and in New Orleans in 1811. In 1822 Denmark Vesey, a freed African American slave, and 36 others were hanged in South Carolina after their planned rebellion was betrayed.

Slaves were not the only workers driven to rebellion because of their working conditions. Indentured servants mutinied in Maine as early as 1636. Later, groups of workingmen united to press for better conditions and organized strikes. For example, New Jersey ironworkers went on strike in 1774. New York printers followed suit in 1778, and sailors and rope makers went on strike in 1779. Many other smaller acts of resistance played a crucial part in establishing the relationship between the underprivileged and the wealthy.

A

THANKSGIVING SERMON,

PREACHED JANUARY 1, 1808,

In St. Thomas's, or the African Episcopal, Church, Philadelphia:

ON ACCOUNT OF

THE ABOLITION

OF THE

AFRICAN SLAVE TRADE,

ON THAT DAY,

BY THE CONGRESS OF THE UNITED STATES.

BY ABSALOM JONES,
RECTOR OF THE SAID CHURCH.

———

PHILADELPHIA:
PRINTED FOR THE USE OF THE CONGREGATION.
FRY AND KAMMERER, PRINTERS.
1808.

ABOVE: **The 1808 thanksgiving sermon given by Absalom Jones, rector of St. Thomas African Episcopal Church in Philadelphia, to celebrate the passing of a law by the U.S. Congress prohibiting the import of slaves into the United States.**

Abolitionist Someone who believed in and worked for doing away with slavery

Acadians French colonists in the New World who settled mostly in Acadia, now the Canadian province of Nova Scotia. More than 5,000 were removed and -resettled by the British after the region was captured during the French and Indian War.

Alms Food or money given to the poor.

Almshouse A privately financed home for the poor. Also known as a poorhouse.

Apprenticeship A contractual agreement under which one person is bound to serve another for a specified length of time in return for training in a skill or trade.

Asylum An institution created to care for the sick and the poor, especially those who were mentally ill.

Charitable society Groups composed of private citizens, often united by a common religion, cultural heritage, or occupation, which collected money from their members and distributed it to the poor and needy.

Discrimination To treat someone unfavorably based on some factor other than individual merit, for example, based on their race, religion, or culture.

Elizabethan Poor Law of 1601 This law created the system on which assistance for the poor in colonial America was based. It said that family had first responsibility for caring for the poor, followed by the church, then the state. It also distinguished between "indoor" and "outdoor" relief, and stressed the importance of residency in determining who was eligible.

Epidemic A contagious disease that infects a disproportionately large part of the population. "Virgin soil epidemics" occur when populations have no previous contact with a disease and no immunity, such as when large numbers of Native Americans were killed by diseases like smallpox and the plague brought to the New World by Europeans.

Indenture A contract binding one person to work for another for a specified period of time.

Indentured servant A person bound by an indenture, usually for four to seven years, in return for specified benefits. The benefits usually included transportation to the New World, food and shelter while under contract, and sometimes money or land at the end of the contract.

Indoor relief Assistance for the poor in the form of housing and support in an institution such as an almshouse or an orphanage. Often provided to children, the elderly, and the sick.

Journeyman A person who has learned a skill or trade and works for another person, usually on a day-job basis.

Outdoor relief Assistance for the poor provided by a town in the form of food, clothes, and money. Usually short term in nature and most often provided to those who wanted but were unable to find work. Persons had to be a resident of the town to qualify.

Piecework Work (often simple manufacturing or construction) for which somebody is paid for each piece completed, not the time spent working.

Poverty The state of lacking the amount of money or material possessions that are considered normal for a minimal existence in a given society. Today poverty is often defined by the government based on a certain annual income level.

ABOVE: **Front view of Dutch-built buildings on Broad and Pearl streets in Lower Manhattan, New York City, around 1820.**

Redemptioners Poor emigrants who traveled to the colonies under a contract that allowed them a set period of time (usually 14 days) after arriving to arrange payment for their transportation. Most could not make payment and were forced to become indentured servants to pay their debt.

Refugee Someone who flees to a foreign country to escape persecution (often religious) or danger (such as during or after a war).

Relief Goods (food, shelter, clothing), services (e.g., medical treatment), or money provided to assist someone in poverty or distress. Modern government sponsored relief is sometimes called "welfare."

Speculation Accumulating title to property (usually land in the colonial era) for the sole purpose of selling it at a profit at a later date.

Tenant farming Renting farmland in return for an agreed-to quantity or percentage of the crops produced by the land. Also called "sharecropping."

Warning out The practice of towns sending away or punishing people who showed no visible means of support, and who were not legal residents of the town. This allowed towns to avoid paying relief to support poor people.

Workhouse Institutions built to house and reform unemployed but able-bodied poor people.

1500

1584	Sir Walter Raleigh lands on Roanoke Island and names the surrounding area Virginia in honor of Queen Elizabeth I, the "virgin queen."
1587	Roanoke Colony is established. By 1590 the settlers of the colony had disappeared.
1606	The London Company sponsors a colonizing expedition to Virginia.
1607	Colonists of the London Company start a settlement at Jamestown in Virginia. By the end of the year starvation and disease reduce the original 105 settlers to just 32 survivors.

1600

1609	The Dutch East India Company sponsors Henry Hudson's voyage of exploration to North America.
1609–1610	Approximately 440 Jamestown settlers die during the "starving time."
1613	A Dutch trading post is set up on lower Manhattan Island.
1616	A smallpox epidemic decimates the Native American population in New England.
1619	Twenty Africans are delivered by a Dutch ship to Jamestown. They are offered for sale as indentured servants, marking the beginning of slavery in colonial America.
1620	November 9, the *Mayflower* lands at Cape Cod, Massachusetts, with 101 colonists.
1623	Dutch colonists, sponsored by the Dutch West India Company, arrive in New Amsterdam, which later becomes New York.
1624	The Virginia Company charter is revoked in London, and Virginia is declared a royal colony.
1630	John Winthrop leads a Puritan migration of 900 colonists to Massachusetts Bay. Boston is established.
1634	First settlement in Maryland.
1635	Boston Latin School is established as the first public school in America.
1641	Slavery becomes legal in New England.
1652	Rhode Island enacts the first law in the colonies banning slavery.
1660	The English monarchy is restored under King Charles II. The Navigation Act requires the exclusive use of English ships for trade in the English colonies and limits exports of tobacco, sugar, and other commodities to England or its colonies.
1663	King Charles II establishes the colony of Carolina.
1664	Dutch colonial governor Peter Stuyvesant surrenders New Amsterdam to the British, who later rename it New York.
1664	Maryland passes a law making lifelong servitude for black slaves mandatory.
1675–1676	King Philip's War erupts in New England between colonists and Native Americans.
1681	Pennsylvania is founded by Quaker William Penn.
1690	King William's War, a conflict in Europe between the French and English, spills over to the colonies.

1700-1800

1700   The European population in the English colonies in America reaches 275,000, with Boston (pop. 7,000) as the largest city, followed by New York (pop. 5,000).

1702–1713   Queen Anne's War begins. The English and American colonists battle the French, their Native American allies, and the Spanish.

1716   The first group of black slaves is brought to the Louisiana Territory.

1720   The population of American colonists reaches 475,000. Boston (pop. 12,000) is the largest city, followed by Philadelphia (pop. 10,000) and New York (pop. 7,000).

1725   The number of black slaves in the mainland American colonies reaches 75,000.

1726   Poor people riot in Philadelphia, tearing down and burning the stocks and pillories.

1730   Baltimore is founded in the Maryland Colony.

1732–1757   Benjamin Franklin publishes *Poor Richard's Almanac*, selling nearly 10,000 copies per year.

1740   King George's War begins, pitting England against France and Spain.

1740   Fifty slaves are hanged in Charleston, South Carolina, after plans for a revolt are revealed.

1752   The first general hospital is founded, in Philadelphia.

1754–1763   The French and Indian War, known as the Seven Years' War in Europe, sees the French and their Algonquin Indian allies fighting the English, aided by the Iroquois, in North America.

1760   The population of colonists in America reaches 1,500,000. In March much of Boston is destroyed by fire.

1763   The Treaty of Paris forces France to give Canada to the British.

1764   The Sugar Act is passed by the English Parliament, increasing duties on imported sugar, textiles, coffee, wines, and indigo (dye). The Currency Act prohibits the colonists from issuing any legal tender paper money.

1765   The Stamp Act imposes the first direct English taxation on the American colonies.

1775–1783   Revolutionary War.

1786   Shays' rebellion in Massachusetts sees angry tenant farmers protesting unfair laws and court system.

1788   The Massachusetts legislature declares the slave trade illegal.

1790   The first census indicates a total population of nearly four million people in the U.S. and western territories. African Americans make up 19 percent of the population, with 90 percent living in the South. Native Americans are not counted.

1812–15   War with Great Britain, now know as the War of 1812, which ends after the signing of the Treaty of Ghent. The conflict fails to resolve the issues that started war, but it begins a long-lasting peace between the United States and Britain.

BOOKS

Berlin, Ira, and Phillip D. Morgan (eds.), *Cultivation and Culture: Labor and the Shaping of Slave Life in the Americas*, Charlottesville: University Press of Virginia, 1993.

Bridenbaugh, Carl, *Cities in Revolt: Urban Life in America, 1743-1776*, Oxford: Oxford University Press, 1970.

Bridenbaugh, Carl, *Cities in the Wilderness: The First Century of Urban Life in America, 1625-1742*, New York: Random House, 1955.

Katz, Michael B., *Poverty and Policy in American History*, New York: Academic Press, 1981.

Kupperman, Karen O., *Indians and English: Facing Off in Early America*, Ithaca, N.Y.: Cornell University Press, 2000.

Mandell, Daniel R., *Behind the Frontier: Indians in Eighteenth-Century Massachusetts*, Lincoln: University of Nebraska Press, 1996.

Smith, Abbot Emerson, *Colonists in Bondage: White Servitude and Convict Labor in America 1607-1776*, Chapel Hill: University of North Carolina, 1947.

Smith, Billy G., *Down and Out in Early America*, College Park: Pennsylvania State University Press, 2004.

Stiverson, Gregory A., *Poverty in a Land of Plenty: Tenancy in Eighteenth Century Maryland*, Baltimore: John Hopkins University Press, 1977.

WEBSITES

"African Americans and the Slave Trade: Africans in America from PBS"
http://www.pbs.org/wgbh/aia/home.html

"The American Colonist's Library"
http://personal.pitnet.net/primarysources/

"The Atlantic Slave Trade and Slave Life in the Americas: A Visual Record"
http://hitchcock.itc.virginia.edu/Slavery/

"Digital History"
http://www.digitalhistory.uh.edu/

"Documenting the American South"
http://docsouth.unc.edu/index.html

"Documents for the Study of American History"
http://www.ukans.edu/carrie/docs/amdocs_index.html

"History Matters"
http://historymatters.gmu.edu/

"Library of Congress American Memory"
http://memory.loc.gov/ammem/

"Mayflower History"
http://www.mayflowerhistory.com/

"Native American History Resources on the Internet"
http://www.hanksville.org/NAresources/indices/NAhistory.html

"The Plymouth Colony Archive Project"
http://etext.lib.virginia.edu/users/deetz/

"Schooling, Education, and Literacy in Colonial America"
http://alumni.cc.gettysburg.edu/~s330558/schooling.html

"Smithsonian Encyclopedia, American Social and Cultural History"
http://www.si.edu/resource/faq/nmah/start.htm

"Virtual Jamestown"
http://www.virtualjamestown.org/page2.html

"The Virtual Library, Unites States History"
http://vlib.iue.it/history/USA/index.html

Page numbers in italic indicate illustrations or maps. Those in bold indicate volume numbers.

Index by Marian Anderson